Contemplations of a Primal Mind

A Florida Sand Dollar Book

Florida Sand Dollar Books

Palmetto Country, by Stetson Kennedy (1989)

Folksongs of Florida, compiled and edited by Alton C. Morris (1990)

Nine Florida Stories by Marjory Stoneman Douglas, edited by Kevin M. McCarthy (1990)

The Camp-Fires of the Everglades: or Wild Sports in the South, by Charles E. Whitehead (1991)

Mullet on the Beach: The Minorcans of Florida, 1768-1788, by Patricia C. Griffin (1991)

Racial Change and Community Crisis: St. Augustine, Florida, 1877-1980, by David R. Colburn (1991)

Flagler: Rockefeller Partner and Florida Baron, by Edward N. Akin (1992)

The Houses of St. Augustine, by Albert Manucy (1992)

The Idea of Florida in the American Literary Imagination, by Anne E. Rowe (1992)

Napoleon Bonaparte Broward: Florida's Fighting Democrat, by Samuel Proctor (1993)

Urban Vigilantes in the New South: Tampa, 1882-1936, by Robert P. Ingalls (1993)

St. Petersburg and the Florida Dream, 1888-1950, by Raymond Arsenault (1996)

Southwest Florida's Wetland Wilderness: Big Cypress Swamp and the Ten Thousand Islands, by Jeff Ripple (1996)

Florida's History Through Its Places: Properties on the National Register of Historic Places, by Morton D. Winsberg (1997)

The Immigrant World of Ybor City: Italians and Their Latin Neighbors in Tampa, 1885-1985, by Gary R. Mormino and George E. Pozzetta (1998)

Some Kind of Paradise, by Mark Derr (1998)

Surrounded on Three Sides, by John Keasler (1999)

Palmetto Leaves, by Harriet Beecher Stowe (1999)

Sunshine States: Wild Times and Extraordinary Lives in the Land of Gators, Guns, and Grapefruit, by Patrick Carr (1999)

Contemplations of a Primal Mind, by Gabriel Horn (2000)

contemplations of
a primal mind

Gabriel Horn
White Deer of Autumn

University Press of Florida
*Gainesville · Tallahassee · Tampa · Boca Raton
Pensacola · Orlando · Miami · Jacksonville*

Copyright 2000 by the Board of Regents of the State of Florida
Originally published 1996 by New World Library
Printed in the United States of America on acid-free paper
All rights reserved

05 04 03 02 01 00   6 5 4 3 2 1

Library of Congress Cataloging-in-Publication Data

Horn, Gabriel, 1947–
Contemplations of a primal mind / Gabriel Horn.
p. cm. — (A Florida sand dollar book)
Originally published: Novato, Calif.: New World Library, c1996.
ISBN 0-8130-1754-8 (alk. paper)
1. Horn, Gabriel, 1947– . 2. Indians of North America—Biography. 3. Indians of
North America—Folklore. I. Title. II. Series.
E90.H67 A3 2000
970.004'97'00922—dc21   99-048441

The University Press of Florida is the scholarly publishing agency for the State
University System of Florida, comprising Florida A&M University, Florida Atlantic
University, Florida International University, Florida State University, University of
Central Florida, University of Florida, University of North Florida, University of
South Florida, and University of West Florida.

University Press of Florida
15 Northwest 15th Street
Gainesville, FL 32611-2079
http://www.upf.com

TABLE OF CONTENTS

DEDICATION

This book is dedicated to the memory of my loving wife, Loon Song (Mongandagwazi).

"Civilized and Primal Thought" was read in its original form to the students and faculty of Virginia Tech University on Columbus Day, 1994. It is dedicated to the Native American students there and to the march they nobly walked on that day for the freedom of American Indian political prisoner Leonard Peltier.

"Original Instruction" is dedicated to the memory of a human sister of the dolphins, Chris Harre of the Dolphin Research Center, Grassy Key, Florida; and to Lori Mazzuca, who brought the dolphins back into my life.

"Paints Her Dreams" for the past and future ghosts of this land. ("Paints Her Dreams" appeared in *Tales from the Great Turtle*, edited by Piers Anthony.)

"Ancestors Among the Stars" for my son, Carises.

"Old Ways" for Calusa, my daughter.

"The Cord" is dedicated to my son, Ihasha.

FOREWORD

I feel very privileged and honored to have been able to read the manuscript of *Contemplations of a Primal Mind* and to have been asked to write the foreword for such a profound and inspiring book. Rarely do I have the opportunity to read a book in which the structure and form of the book are congruent with the message. Gabriel Horn (White Deer of Autumn) has not only given us unique information about "civilized" and "primal" minds, he has given us the opportunity to have the experience of his subject matter in the process of our reading. This experience of congruence itself is worth the reading — and there is so much more.

This book is not just a book about what we think, which is important, it is also a book about how we think, which is even more important. Gabriel Horn clearly states that the way we perceive the world may not be as much a racial distinction as it is an attitudinal difference.

I am reminded of the word that the old Hawaiians (still used today) had for white Westerners, *haole*. When the Western Europeans first invaded the Hawaiian islands, they observed that the Hawaiians started their day with what appeared to be a kind of movement meditation similar to T'ai Chi, which the Hawaiians called the "Ha" or breath of God. The white people or civilized people did not have the "Ha" or were without the breath of God, therefore haole. In Gabriel Horn's terms, "civilized" people are those who have forgotten the Original Instruction or who have lost touch with the Original Instruction. Primal minds know the oneness of all things. Primal minds have maintained an awareness of the oneness of all things and operate from that knowing.

As Horn's Uncle Nippawanock has pointed out, "The word civilized is not synonymous with 'virtuous' or 'honorable' or 'trustworthy,' rather, it is merely indicative of 'having an advanced culture' and 'advanced' is synonymous with 'technological'...." An old Australian aboriginal elder and priest said to me, "Centuries ago you white people decided to go the way of science and technology, and they will destroy the planet. We only hope you realize this before it's too late." *Contemplations of a Primal Mind* is a loving attempt to help us realize the dangers of the choices Western civilization has made.

In his book *In the Absence of the Sacred* Jerry Mander explores the dangers of technology. He gives us a convincing argument that technology as we know it is destructive. Mander confronts us with the excuse we have used to let all kinds of technology proliferate: We tell ourselves that technology is not necessarily bad; it is the way we use it that determines its effect. (I have, I must confess, succumbed to that argument myself.) Mander points out that most modern technology was developed for war and converted for public — I refuse to use the word peaceful here — use to sell it, that the public has never been adequately informed of the strengths and dangers of each new technology, and that, lastly, almost every technology is inherently dangerous in that toxic waste is a necessary by-product of its manufacture. Just as I was struggling to imagine a technology-free world, a group of native elders using their primal minds shared with me that the problem was not technology, per se, but that Western culture did not have adequate spiritual development to produce a technology that would support and enhance wholeness. Western culture has lost touch with our "Original Instruction" and, therefore, cannot develop appropriate technology.

Gabriel Horn, with this book, points us in a direction that will make much of what we experience make sense to us. By helping us to see what has happened to the nature of human intellect, he offers new options. For example, I have long observed that we live in an illusionary world. We have constructed a world built on the illusion of control, the illusion of objectivity, the illusion of perfectionism. We have built this world on intellectual constructs projected onto others and the world around us. We have a virtual reality we call reality, a reality we can no longer perceive or touch. In approaching this virtual reality from the perspective of the primal mind, and observing the civilized mind from that perspective, we have a chance to breathe again.

The Maori are now coming forth and speaking of the *Waitaha*, a peaceful civilization that existed in New Zealand before the war canoes came. This civilization consisted of tribes of people from the world over who lived in harmony with each other, with nature, with the Creator, and with all things. Knowledge of this civilization has been withheld and suppressed, but is now coming forth. The elders of many nature peoples have said, "Our myths and legends have told us that a time would come when we had to come forth and speak in order to save the planet — and that time is now." *Contemplations of a Primal Mind* is a part of that voice. These voices are lovingly calling us to our Original Instruction.

Anne Wilson Schaef, Ph.D.
Honorary Doctorate in Human Letters
Author of *Meditations for Women Who Do Too Much*
and *Native Wisdom for White Minds*

PREFACE

*Until the lion can speak his part, tales of the hunt will
be told by the hunter.*

— African folk saying

Maybe you too stir uneasy with concern over the
welfare of the earth. Maybe you too feel as I do
regarding the behavior of our human species toward
other life forms, each other, and the natural world. And
perhaps, like me, you revolt whenever you hear or read
about oil spills, disappearing wetlands, raped mountains, radioactive dumps, and the man-made laws and
policies designed to pad the pockets, fatten the bank
accounts, and protect the rights of the industrial, corporate, civilized man.

As I travel through the autumn of my life, I've begun
the disturbing realization that even though my Native
American identity could never allow me an active role in
today's environmental destruction, that identity does
not exempt me from the historic judgment that will
befall our species some day. To acknowledge that I share

in that history has both terrified and enraged me. Until recently, I had always thought — or at least hoped — that the earth and the universe exempted certain people from the inevitable results of the mindless destruction enacted by the forces of civilization.

Even more unnerving to me now is seeing the participation in our environmental holocaust by descendants of the Red race people with whom I am identified. For Native Americans serve as guardians of the natural world, or so I thought.

With whatever awareness and insights I've gained in the half century of my life, I've explored the plausible reasons for humanity's free-fall from grace.

First I spoke about these things, and now I'm writing about them. They are the *Contemplations of a Primal Mind*.

The book's first chapter, "Civilized and Primal Thought," deals with my explanation of the two distinct thought processes of civilized and primal peoples. In this chapter I hope to bring those of us with like minds closer, and set into motion thought forms that can help fight the cancer of civilization. I also hope to show that the way I have been taught and have learned to perceive the world may not be a racial distinction, but rather an attitudinal one, thereby reinforcing the indigenous understanding that though we are culturally and racially unique, we are all children of Mother Earth and we all share the responsibility for her well-being.

Chapter two, "Original Instruction," further explores perceptions of our world and reflects that perhaps all of us in our primordial beginnings were encoded with the knowledge of how to live in harmony within our diverse environments. From the memories stored in our collective unconscious, to the recollections of our dim past, our survival as a species depends on the emergence of our Original Instruction. To help illustrate this understanding, I describe the experiences I had with dolphins in the Florida Keys. Hopefully, those times I spent at the Dolphin Research Center will help evoke in your hearts and minds a touch of the wonder and joy, the humility and pride, the will and determination we need to continue as a species on this earth.

Then, through the apparition of an Indian maiden in chapter three, "Paints Her Dreams" reveals our human need for cultural, spiritual, and literal connections to the past. The concept of Peace Day allows us to rediscover bits and pieces of primal wisdom that enable us to live on through the lives of our children, and in the living memories of those we love.

In chapter four, "Ancestors Among the Stars," I guide us out of this world on a quest to better understand and acknowledge the presence of the Star People in our lives. Through a pre-Columbian love story, I invite you to journey with me toward the constellation called the Pleiades. Perhaps, through this chapter and the stories of the present and past within it, our sacred relationship to the stars will not merely be considered, but realized.

Because story is so much a living part of the Primal Mind, chapter five, "Old Ways," tells of an eerie and true account of those who are born with the sixth finger. By introducing you to two of my wife's relatives and their experiences in and out of this dimension, and by once again attempting to put the oral tradition into written form, may I evoke the primal connection and power of the "Old Ways."

It is fitting that *Contemplations of a Primal Mind* closes with an essay based on maintaining the Old Ways in this civilized world. The final chapter, "The Cord," reveals the ways and practices we have passed on to our children can allow our survival despite the spirit-killers of the civilized world who threaten to steal both the Old Ways and the future.

May the primal thought articulated and described in *Contemplations of a Primal Mind* bring us closer together, so we may be of one mind and heart in defending and loving our Mother, the earth.

CHAPTER 1

Civilized and Primal Thought

The word civilized is not synonymous with "virtuous" or "honorable" or "trustworthy;" rather, it is merely indicative of "having an advanced culture," and "advanced" is synonymous with "technological...."

— Thomas E. Sanders (Nippawanock)
Literature of the American Indian

"Civilized man seems a curious creature to primitive man, who would not wantonly trade places with him because the resultant loss would be too great." Twenty years ago, when my Uncle Nippawanock first wrote this statement in the college text and anthology *Literature of the American Indian*, I became aware of the thought processes that separate two distinct ways of perceiving the universe and life itself.

Civilized and primitive — they are specific terms that often measure, and sometimes even define, the nature of human intelligence; the former bonded to the technology from whence it sprang, the latter intertwined with the natural world from whence it evolved. For most people the word "civilized" implies an acceptable level of social etiquette and sophisticated thought. It indicates clean and organized ways of living. The word "primitive" seldom suggests the same. Though the denotative meanings of each word prove neither implication is correct, it's difficult to discuss the two without conjuring up the stereotypical connotations and the images they perpetuate.

At an early stage of my life, when I first formed many of my worldly impressions, I had absorbed into my perceptions of the world caricatures of primal-thinking people. My recollections of those images reveal my own superficial picture of what primal people were like, and seem prejudicial at best. Though a few generations of children have been educated after me, it doesn't shock me to hear my students today express similar superficial ideas.

"Are you civilized or primitive?" This is one of the first questions I pose to students when I begin teaching a course in Native American literature. Whether they are in elementary school, middle school, high school, college, or graduate school, their responses are generally alike. It's not unusual for them to recoil like offended rattlers at any inference that might connect them to the word primitive. In their civilized minds no ties exist between them and that word.

Whether they speak in simple sentences or complex

explanations, their reactions, in a curious way, are strangely similar. They often associate the word primitive with scantily clothed two-leggeds bearing crude instruments usually described as "spears," "clubs," or even "big sticks." They think of a primitive man heading for his cave with a slain bloody animal slung over his shoulder.

During an opening discussion about primitive people, an artistic college sophomore sketched his idea of primitive man to help his classmates visualize the concept. Since he illustrated for the college newspaper, his drawing drew other students to his desk. His picture depicted a burly, scraggly-bearded, wiry-haired, hunched-over man standing by a fire clutching a club. A horizontal pole suspended by two vertical poles supported a small animal resembling a fox or rabbit, roasting over the open fire. In his other hand, the beast-like man clasped the long, thickly matted hair of an especially endowed, bare-breasted and unconscious woman.

Though the picture evoked some laughter, the humor and the concept it springs from indicate to a large extent how civilized humans see themselves in relation to others and to the world in which they live. It's easy to see that male superiority and female servitude have been well-established in the minds of most of my contemporary students, regardless of age and education level.

Yet not all of my students picture the primitive in such a repressed and silly state. The ones who see themselves as liberal and open-minded, for example, applaud themselves for being better aware of sexual and racial stereotyping. Yet in the next breath they express their concerns for the lesser-developed peoples of the world who have yet to achieve "our level of technology." And as sincere as they are, like many of the others, they too focus on physical characteristics or appearance. They too imagine primitive people as long-haired, shadowy figures.

Most of my students' conception of primitive life shows people living in crude cave-like dwellings at the base of a mountain or on the side of a high cliff. Some in every class think of primitive people living in tepees or tents. They imagine primitive men carrying rocks and spears, chasing animals across a wild and threatening landscape. A few include bows and arrows as part of the primal arsenal. And even though some of these images may be somewhat realistic, ideas regarding primitive people's livelihood remain unexplored and unknown.

Anthropological and historical institutions of Western thought still perpetuate the notion of a primal mind comprehending little beyond a hunter-gatherer existence. Sketchings of Indians in a Smithsonian book I remember seeing as a boy pictured colorful hunting and gathering scenes where men raise their spears at the monstrous mammoth, while across the page women pick berries from nearby bushes. These are the simplistic images that still linger in our childhood memories.

Most of my students are not aware of and don't understand the primal mind's ability to abstract. Yet what could be more challenging than creating the petroglyphs of Canyon de Chelly or as intriguing as a Mayan Indian observatory? The concept of Wah-kon-tah, the Great Holy Mystery, for example, was and still is too much of an abstraction for most civilized people to accept. Such a concept of a universal Prime Mover or First Cause was far too abstract for the first Europeans who landed in the Americas. As a result of their inability to see beyond an anthropomorphic God, they created the "Great Spirit," when attempting to understand the primal Indian concept of the First Cause. The Great Spirit meshed better with the Judeo-Christian idea of God.

The concept of the Great Holy Mystery is but one example of a primal mind's remarkable ability to abstract and concentrate. To meditate on the idea of the sacred circle and cycles of time, or to wonder about the stars and one's relationship to them and to nature, provides a keen sensitivity, a conscious closeness with the unseen powers.

> I, Nezahualcoyotl, ask this:
> Is it true one really lives on the earth?
> Not forever on the earth,
>   only a little while here.
> Though it be jade it falls apart,
> though it be gold it wears away,
> though it be quetzal plumage it is
>   torn asunder.
> Not forever on the earth,
>   only a little while here....

> — From the poet-king
> Nezahualcoyotl (1402-1472)

Such a philosophical observation of the world reveals a mind that recognizes both the splendor and mortality of the human experience. Such a simple poem presents an idea as abstract and sophisticated as those other seemingly simple stick drawings of stars and other shapes left on the stone walls of time. The very idea of humans contemplating the stars....

The rock drawings of our ancient ancestors were some of my earliest remembered images. It's as though they etch themselves into our minds because they stimulate something old in us. They were drawn, I imagine, because the artists wanted us to be aware that others existed before us. This was something left of their world, something from their minds that they chose to leave, to live on.

As I scanned a rock wall one spring morning near Zuni, New Mexico, I wondered about the people who lived in those apartment-like dwellings carved out of the rock, molded into the plateau. While looking at the hollowed rooms through the empty windows, I got the feeling that these folks had lived there a long, long time. Yet some of the first words I remember associating with primitive people were words like "nomadic" and "wandering." Though so little is known about these ancient people, I know one thing for certain: the people who painted on those rocks and who lived in those pueblos were not "wanderers." They existed as a well-rooted society with sophisticated social order, and without armies, police, or prisons.

Yet the civilized mind abolishes any concept of

primitive people existing as a nation, yesterday or today. Primitive people are not allowed the right to occupy a country with boundaries. They cannot have a land base that belongs to them. The civilized mind denies primitive people any recognition of nationhood. The students of civilized education learn at an early age to see primitive people much like they do herds of "wild" animals, always chasing an elusive food source and wandering about in bands. It is easy to understand where these ideas come from. The U.S. Immigration & Naturalization Service recommends a pamphlet by D. L. Hennessey to all persons filing applications to become U.S. citizens in California. Published in 1969 in Berkeley, California, the pamphlet reads: "A few hundred years ago there were no white people in this country. The only inhabitants in the U.S. were the Indians. These Indians usually lived in small bands and wandered about from place to place. They lived mostly by hunting and fishing. They were often quarrelsome. Some of the different tribes or bands had settled homes and were partly civilized, but most of them were wandering savages who did nothing to develop this great country." The INS still handed these things out to people at least through the 1970s, possibly later.

Where have these "savages" wandered from? Where do they wander to? The accepted beliefs of Western civilized scientists regarding the origin and migration of the indigenous people of the Americas perpetuates the idea that Native Americans descended from prehistoric apes in Africa, who propagated and evolved, migrated into Asia, and eventually wandered across a land bridge to North America.

Commonly referred to as the Bering Strait theory, this notion of migratory nomadism has become so embedded in the civilized institutions of science and history that, for many, it is accepted as truth and taught as fact.

According to *Red Earth, White Lies* by Vine Deloria Jr., a leading voice for Native Americans of this century, the American Indian Science and Engineering Society has sponsored a series of conferences on traditional knowledge of Indian tribes. This knowledge, along with recent scientific evidence, archeological findings, and geological information, challenges the status quo doctrine relating to the origin and migration of Native American ancestors. Yet the considerations of other origin and migratory possibilities based on understandings gathered from objective scientific inquiry and on knowledge acquired from accumulated primal wisdom often evokes a defensive resistance from civilized-thinking men that borders on hostility.

It appears that the established institutions of Western science continue to disregard the ancient knowledge and spiritual insights found in Native American creation accounts, as well as the information and wisdom contained within other forms of indigenous oral and written literature. Because of this neglect, the primal mind can only assume that the civilized ideas of origin and migration involve ulterior motives that go beyond pure science. And unless the civilized mind exposes itself to other perspectives and becomes willing to listen to ancient voices, then the primal mind can only perceive Western ethnocentrism as a rationalization to occupy the land of indigenous people throughout this hemisphere and also a justification to disenfranchise them of culture.

But perhaps the most insulting assumption Western civilized science has ever inflicted on the indigenous people of the Americas are the implications contained in the definitive and implied meanings associated with the word "wandering."

The Native American literature students in my classes who shared similar stereotypes of primal man had never been exposed to any of the important traditions and teachings of the original inhabitants of this continent. The eloquent Iroquois' *Epic of Deganawida*, for example, tells the story of the virgin-born Peacemaker and the forming of the Iroquois Confederacy. These students never had the moving experience of hearing or reading of the great orator Hyonwatha's journey, and never learned how Deganawida and Hyonwatha helped establish the Law of Great Peace among the Hodenosaunee (The League of the Iroquois Five Nations). These students know nothing of the League's longevity, that it is the oldest established peace among nations in the world, the first United Nations in the world.

It was under this Law of Great Peace that the original thirteen colonies were protected and later formed. The Law's makers modeled a constitution of their own, from which the very symbols of contemporary

American freedom were taken. The white-headed eagle clutches the arrows in his talons that represent each of the five nations; now there are thirteen arrows for the original English colonies. But the pine bough, the Iroquois symbol of peace, was changed to an olive branch because Benjamin Franklin wanted something that represented peace with a European symbol.

Another example of primal achievement that has become historically obscure to civilized man is the awesome complex called Pueblo Bonito, in northwest New Mexico. It was the largest apartment-like complex in the world until the twentieth century, yet it was far more connected to the web of life than the one that rivaled it in New York City. In Pueblo Bonito, which was one of a dozen of its kind, everything was in alignment with the phases of Moon, the directions of the Earth, and positions of the Sun. Each living quarter had its own kiva, a small circular room for prayer and meditation.

From the pre-Columbian ruins like those found at Pueblo Bonito to the Calusa mounds discovered near the Everglades 1,500 miles away, all over the Western Hemisphere indigenous people enjoyed the security and social activity that occurs when large numbers of like-minded individuals live close to each other and their environment. These places exist as ancient reminders of a primal way of life that allowed humans to flourish, yet kept them connected to the natural world they lived in. That connection to their environment is the kind of relationship that enabled primal people to evolve peacefully and in harmony with their world. When Columbus first landed in this hemisphere, he wrote: "Their manners are praiseworthy and generous.... They freely give what they have. And their discourse is ever gentle and always accompanied with a smile...."

That first encounter between the newly emerging civilized mind of the European and the ancient primal mind of the Native American intrigued other observers and recorders of the time.

Bartolome De Las Casas was the first Catholic priest ordained in the "New World." He served as a chaplain on a Spanish expedition in 1502, and for his services was granted land and slaves. He rejected the idea of slavery, however, and protested against Spanish cruelty for the remainder of his long life. In one of his records he describes the native people shortly after Spanish contact: "They are by nature the most humble, patient, and peaceable, holding no grudges, free from embroilment, neither excitable nor quarrelsome. These people are the most devoid of rancor, hatred, or desire for vengeance of any people in the world."

Yet, almost without exception, whenever I pose the question, "Are you civilized or primitive?" to my students, without hesitation and further deliberation, they usually respond in union and camaraderie. Some nod their heads reassuringly to each other. Others smile and roll their eyes. For even the suggestion of being primitive falls just short of an insult. They assume their condition as a human birthright. Perhaps they're correct, for it is, in fact, the way they were raised to think and behave. "We're civilized!" they proclaim proudly.

It is at this moment that class has officially begun, for I have poured their preconceived ideas about civilized and primal people into the false foundation on which they have grown somewhat uncomfortable and insecure about themselves. And like I once had, they too grow more curious about Uncle Nippawanock's words: "Civilized man seems a curious creature to primitive man who would not wantonly trade places with him, because the resultant loss would be too great."

Since language expresses and reflects human world views and attitudes, and since we are communicating in English, I have chosen to use the word primal in place of primitive whenever discussing the thought process of indigenous people, or any people living in harmony with their natural environment. As Newberry Award-winning writer Jamake Highwater puts it: "The term primal doesn't carry with it all the negative baggage of implied meanings." Instead, it is a word that adds a freshness to the old proven ways of thinking. And it is the word best suited for the purposes of discussing human thought. Thus, 'civilized' and 'primal' are not words that define the superiority or the inferiority of different types of human intelligence, but rather terms that, when fairly presented, provide a better understanding of the diverse and diametrically opposed processes of human thought.

As a result of the ignorance and confusion surrounding primal people, who are usually the indigenous inhabitants of any particular land that civilized man desires or is presently living on, land is usurped. It is subtly taken away. Or it is openly stolen.

The missionaries are usually the first to go into the primal communities. Their job undermines primal religion, they create social disorder, carrying with them the civilized diseases for which the native people have little or no resistance. Other times land is usurped more blatantly. When the Supreme Court of the United States ruled that the Cherokee Nation was a sovereign nation, more forceful measures were required to steal their land as the avarice of civilized men became uncontrollable. Civilized men had discovered "the metal that makes them crazy." All that was needed was sanction from the commander-in-chief of the armed forces.

And even though the sovereignty of the Cherokee people had met American civilized standards, these standards didn't matter, because of greed.

The achievements of the Cherokee people regarding language, however, warrant admiration and respect. They printed and published their native language and every man, woman, and child was able to become literate in a foreign language (English) within ten years — something no other nation had or has ever done. The Cherokee also adopted a constitution and form of government that resembled that of the United States. They even had churches!

The Supreme Court ruling stated that the citizens of Georgia and the United States had no authority to enter the boundaries defined as the Cherokee Nation without expressed consent of the Cherokee people.

But this Supreme Court decision would hold no weight heavier than the paper it was written on. President Andrew Jackson, now appropriately pictured on a twenty-dollar bill and honored with statues and parades from Washington, D.C. to Florida, told Supreme Court Justice John Marshall that Marshall himself should go down to Georgia and enforce the decision of a free and independent Cherokee Nation.

Of course, Chief Justice Marshall couldn't do that, for the president is commander-in-chief of the armed forces. He has the guns. So, for the first and only time in United States history, a president overruled a Supreme Court decision, and sent his army to Cherokee land. And wherever a civilized army goes, it appears that so goes what is decent about being human.

On what was later romanticized as the "Trail of Tears," to reflect the sorrow of those who witnessed the horror, the Cherokee people were forced on a death march. Within weeks after their eviction from their homeland, a fourth of the Cherokee nation died. So many died that the soldiers would only let them bury their dead every third day. The late oral historian and writer Forrest Carter described how husbands carried their dead wives, mothers carried their dead babies, brothers carried their dead sisters. They would lie down by the corpses at night and rise to carry them again the next day.

Primal people, those tribes and nations who have always retained their Original Instruction and Purpose as a people, have lived close to the earth and in harmony with their environment from antiquity. They are the ones too often regarded as the obstacles in the place of what civilized man desires. So they must go. As a civilized United States general once said, "The only good Indian is a dead one."

The removal or extinction is carried out by whatever method is devised by the militarily superior civilized nation. It happened then, and it happens today, all over the world. The Sami (also known as Laplanders) know how Norway came into existence. The Maori know the way New Zealand was created. Just ask the Aborigines of Australia. They know what civilization did when it invaded the body of their mother and their lands. It's as though civilized-thinking men are cancerous cells invading the body of the earth. Wherever they travel, they consume what is beneficial to her body, create an imbalance in the ecosystem, and eventually self-destruct.

Among most civilized nations today, the divine rights to "subdue" and "dominate" allow credence to the self-proclaimed idea of Manifest Destiny. And like the land on which they live, the indigenous, primal people become the victims. They must conform to the technological whims and demands of civilization. They must accept the proselytizing religious dogma or governmental ideology that accompanies the invasion. And they must especially conform to civilized thought — and do it quickly, or they are simply sacrificed.

Those primal-thinking survivors who find themselves living in square houses, driving to work in cars, and sitting in front of the television news at night must struggle to retain any primal thought. They must struggle against consumer mentality and state-imposed ideology.

Too often primal voices become quiet. Few still sing the songs to help the crops grow — food can be bought at the supermarket. Few still sing the incantations and perform the rituals for healing and for life. The people now have doctors practicing western medicine, and the commercial rituals of Christmas. The once primal-thinking people don't need to apologize and explain to the plant nations why their lives must be taken for sustenance and good health — drugs are available at drug stores. It doesn't take but a single generation to lose its connectedness to the environment and the world around them. If the moon waxes and wanes without experiencing the loving vibration of song and dance, if honor and respect are no longer directed toward the sun, if positive, loving vibrations no longer course through the air and beyond, the primal mind is dead.

Buy this, buy that, buy now! Buy and save! These are the vibrations now jamming the space where sound travels, and when this barrage of consumer advertising becomes a motivating force in their lives, primal people will be no more. For then they will live the way of civilization. Consume. Consume. Consume. A great Lakota holy man, John Fire Lame Deer, once wrote that civilized humans were "bred to be consumers."

Of course, with consumption comes the need for money. So primal people must get jobs and learn to work in the civilized way, without fun, too often without heart, without bliss. They work by the clock on artificial time. If they can't or won't do it, they are regarded as failures, lost in the new civilized world, incapable of adapting. Many become addicted to alcohol. Lives are destroyed. Some kill themselves. They kill each other. Then the land that was in their care and keeping is turned over to the civilized-thinking men who tear it apart. The trees are destroyed; the air is polluted. All for money.

Puppet tribal authorities collude with government and corporate interests and lease native lands. Many of the leaseholders farm the land excessively. Because the civilized mind is not satisfied with enough to live comfortably, they grow all the crops they possibly can to buy things — the materialistic things that define civilization. It's the American way. But often the crops the farmers grow are not indigenous and they either require more water than the land can supply or they spoil from too much water. This kind of farming requires irrigation, or drainage of the land, as well as massive quantities of insecticides to protect the harvest from infestation. Of course there are the ranchers too. As new leaseholders they transform forests to pastures. They graze imported cattle, and in a short time they leave the land eroded and dry, desolate, and undesirable.

Exxon, Peabody, and others like them, are another kind of leaseholder. They are corporate oil companies that drill deep into the land. Coal and other mineral companies make whole mountains disappear or gouge out huge gaping holes in the land. They pollute the running waters of the earth with residue and waste. Lumber companies rape entire forests. Developers exploit the natural beauty of the land. They see it as expendable, depleting natural resources and contaminating local estuaries, rivers, streams, and salt water bays with sewage and run-off.

If we could ask a Yanomani about primal and civilized thought, one who hasn't succumbed to some missionary's disease or fallen victim to the guns of desperadoes looking for gold in the rain forests and the easy way through the civilized door, I wonder what a Yanomani would say? How would he explain the difference between civilized and primal thought? I wonder what a Sami would say. I wonder what a Maori would say. Or an Australian Aborigine. A Mandingo. I'm sure they too have tried to understand how the chasm between thought processes occurred. Perhaps they too have discovered something from such a quest. Perhaps their struggle to understand posed many questions to them. A few questions in particular may have lingered, beckoning to be understood.

When did we separate? When did humanity begin to lose that concept of a Totality — a Oneness that is all things living together? When did some of us stop regarding the Earth as Mother?

Perhaps primal people still living would need a sacred fire to expound on such an idea. Perhaps they would need to fast and pray for such understanding. They would have to observe for many years. Then they would need a circle of people to help them articulate what they learned. Perhaps then they would begin by saying, it happened a long time ago.

In the primordial evolution of humankind, a definite separation in ways of thinking has occurred. I believe it is fair to assume that this separation was not present in the beginning when humans sought only to survive. Could it be possible that this separation occurred when our ancestors created tools, or artificial extensions, to forge out their existence?

Though these extensions gave them physical equality among the other life forms, humans had yet to make the separation that resulted in civilized thought. They used spears and bows, for example, to kill other animals. They shaped other implements to utilize what they killed. They cultivated crops and invented tools to help them. They even made the wheel — the more civilized Romans used it as a tool of colonization and conquest; the more primal-thinking Mayans made toys for their children. Regardless of their uses, the result was the birth of technology. It sprang from the most basic of these artificial extensions.

But something curious, if not mysterious, happened to the nature of human intellect. It can be seen in something as simple as the different ways that the Romans and the Mayans used the wheel. For it is here that civilized and primitive thought split into two ways of thinking and, like a great river, branched into two different directions.

In one direction flows the River of Time and Knowing. It's the thought process that adheres to our Original Instruction: Take only what you need, live in harmony and balance with your environment, love the Earth. Such a thought process doesn't allow artificial extensions, like the tools we create or even the weapons we make, to become actual extensions of the self. For the people whose thought process swims along this river of knowledge do not feel that any artificial extension makes them superior to other life forms. Thus the wheel is sacred, as it symbolizes the wholeness and oneness of all things. Its four quarters represent the diversity and balance in the universe. It provides understanding and spiritual growth. This foundation of thought creates the primal-thinking mind.

Civilized man takes a different turn here, only he runs aground. He does not flow on the River of Time and Knowing. He travels on an asphalt road, and it is along this newly defined way that he seems to have intellectually severed his ties with the primal mind. Maybe it's at this point that he becomes mutated or transformed, as actor Dustin Hoffman once stated in a TV interview about the movie *Outbreak*, into a "virus infecting the earth." For the civilized men and women who travel this course of intellect assume that their artificial extensions, which they have become so dependent upon, have become actual extensions of themselves, and they begin to separate, not only from their primal counterparts, but from other life forms as well. They regard the wheel not as something sacred, but solely as an instrument to serve them — to make life physically easier, to move faster.

The resultant loss is, indeed, too great for primal-thinking people who still regard the animals and birds, the plants and the trees, and all other life forms great and small as relatives who share a common origin and mother — the earth.

In order to become civilized, humans not only disregard their collective past, they abandon the concept of Wah-kon-tah. Civilized man no longer regards the earth as a living cosmic entity that binds him into an interrelationship with all other life forms. Civilized man regards the earth not as the great mother that the primal Tsalgi (Cherokee) call Monalah, but as a planet, an object created for civilized man's use. Even his language becomes a technological achievement used to acquire power rather than receive it, for his language objectifies not only the earth but the entire universe as well.

Consequently, civilized man does what he wants, when he wants. His greatest achievement is his technological ability to alter the environment — that natural world where all forms of life live and die. Unlike primal people, who sought and still seek to adapt to their natural surroundings, civilized man changes the environment to suit himself. He may have an air-conditioned mall in the heat of a south Florida summer, or a warm athletic dome in the frigid winters of Minnesota, but the power demand that creates such artificially controlled abominations is so great that the natural environments they depend upon are altered to the point of ruin. This lack of regard for the balance of nature becomes acceptable behavior because civilized man has separated himself from nature. But this he does only in his civilized, thinking mind.

Because of the nature of his intellect, civilized man does not stop here. He regards himself as a superior creature, and as such, civilized man can now kill beyond the need to survive. He has, as Uncle Nip asserted, "an intellectually developed killer instinct." Civilized man kills for sport and amusement, and for political and even religious reasons. He kills his own species en masse. And he can abuse, experiment on, and destroy all other life forms. He has become, as the poet e.e. cummings wrote, "Manunkind."

And though civilized man is still as much of a territorial creature as his primal brother, his artificial extensions of war have aided his instinct for aggression and caused him to vastly expand his greed for territory. He has become ruthless: ruthless to his fellow man, ruthless to the earth. His modern industrial civilizations have been described by leading world biologists today as cancers on the body of the earth. And, like cancers, they attack the healthy living cells, and the vital organs, like the Florida Everglades, with urban sprawls of human waste and contamination. They eat their way through the rain forests of the world, destroying the indigenous protectors along the way.

Maybe Dustin Hoffman was right about humans being a virus infecting the earth, but I believe that statement should be qualified and not so generalized as to lump all of humanity together, though I'm sure that is how time will record us as a species. Not all humans are "the virus" or the cancerous cells destroying the planet as we know her — it's the civilized humans.

A primal man kills to survive. He may even own a gun, but the nature of his intellect does not allow him to assume that because he has the gun, he is a superior creature. And, if he must kill, it is out of need and need only that he does, for he still retains his ties to the natural, "technologically unimproved" world where all things are interrelated, where all life forms are his relatives.

Perhaps one example of this concept of interrelatedness is how the Plains Indian developed the art of counting coups. The idea of counting coups came from the practice of not killing in battle. It was rather the delivery of a swift blow or strike with a coup stick to an opponent's vital area to render the victim humiliated. That humiliation, though painfully and embarrassingly inflicted, would force him off the battlefield a loser — but he was alive! Occasionally a warrior would die of such a wound in territorial conflict, but not often. The primary intent in battle was not to kill — until the civilized Americans arrived with guns.

But the true glory of winning the prized eagle feather among the Plains warriors in battle did not render women without husbands, children without fathers, mothers without sons.

The constant changing of territorial boundaries and the subsequent skirmishes that resulted when words failed give us an example of how the primal mind evolved in a way that allowed it to fulfill its needs without destroying life. Some of their people's greatest teachers were other life forms of the earth, like the birds and the other animals, even insects. They too had territories and territorial skirmishes. They still do. But they do not kill en masse to conquer. This idea of counting coups was another evolutionary leap for the primal mind.

Similar evolutions of thought occurred among indigenous and uncivilized people all over the world. They recognized their connection to the universe — it alone being described as an incomprehensible totality which enabled them to see themselves and regard themselves as an equal part of an unimaginable whole. They viewed themselves as superior to nothing, yet a part of everything — a concept that creates humility and pride simultaneously.

The military appropriation of the lands of indigenous people and the attempted, and often successful, genocide of those people and their way of life by the more civilized can, in part, be attributed to the allegiance of civilized man to a god that he created in his own image — a civilized, anthropomorphic god, a supreme being removed from nature, praised with pious words and violent acts.

Civilized man created a dogma that produced organized religions that instructed the practitioners to "subdue" and "dominate" all life forms — ironically, even the earth, especially that earth inhabited by others. The theft of the Western Hemisphere can historically be partially attributed to diseases brought by the invading European civilizations. But civilized diseases were only accomplices to the gun, the most significant artificial extension of civilized man's inventiveness. For it is the curious nature of his intellect that makes it possible for him to believe that it is the gun that allows him his greatest sense of superiority.

However, should civilized man suffer the loss of the artificial extensions that have temporarily allowed him physical superiority, he would be in a lesser state of existence — at least physically — than the "inferior" life forms who he had originally sought to merely live among. Without his artificial extensions, he would be in a lesser position than those primal peoples he now regards himself as separated from and superior to.

What would happen if the plug were suddenly pulled on electricity? It's a question I often pose to my students of Native American literature. If civilized man were to experience this for any extended period of time, what would the July heat be like in one of Miami's glass buildings? How will the civilized world function when the earth runs out of oil and becomes depleted of coal? Beer will become warm in the refrigerator. Ice cream will melt. Meats will decay. Gas pumps won't work. Planes will sit idly at airports all over the world. Cars will remain parked. There will be riots. Looting. Raping. Have we forgotten the "great blackout" that occurred in the Northeast in the sixties? Do we remember the famous photograph in *Life* magazine of rush hour at Grand Central Station in New York City when the electricity went dead? Civilized man appeared lost. Anxious. Despairing. The very thought that civilized man should be without artificial extensions, or the "progress" fueled by these natural resources, is a thought he dares not entertain.

So his civilized response, and the one most commonly made by students, is that "tomorrow will be better." Should the ozone depletion become so great that humans can no longer expose themselves to natural sunlight, civilized man seems unconcerned. After all, in the turmoil of his irrational reasoning, the civilized, thinking mind believes that tomorrow, "science" will be able to fix it. And if that doesn't work, he'll build boxes that emanate artificial sunlight, and temporarily seek contentment and warmth inside those boxes, one giant mall and condominium complex after the other. Civilized man must go forth, heading toward some technological utopia, sometime, somewhere in the future.

Unfortunately, the balance of life as we know it is at stake. So the indigenous, primal-thinking people struggle to maintain a state of inner peace and spirituality against an unrelenting assault on the earth. And it is a struggle met courageously and often horribly, as the recent slaughter of Yanomani and other primal peoples reveals. It is a heart-rending struggle that even my wife, Simone, faced as she battled the technologically influenced, civilized disease of breast cancer. Yet, somehow the primal mind seeks to retain a state of inner peace and spirituality, for he and she are yet bound to the "technologically unimproved world" that they still call Mother Earth.

This sense of spiritual contentment is the real peace. Black Elk described it as "the peace that comes within the souls of men when they realize their relationship, their oneness, with the universe and all its powers, and when they realize that at the center of the universe dwells Wakan-Tanka, and that this center is really everywhere, it is within each of us."

Such peace is not realized within civilized man who, as if driven by his own insecurities, continues to pave over old graves and destroy Old Ways. He must create that superhighway to the Promised Land — only the Promised Land becomes an impossible dream, for it is a forever unfulfilling materialistic world. In this process of trying to achieve the unattainable technological utopia, he sacrifices the "real peace," for he cannot know what it's like to live in harmony with himself and his environment. And he can't be happy, for he can't live happily in an artificial environment. His technology of artificial and self-weakening tools has become a barrier that separates him from the natural world, and he cannot respond naturally to an artificial world. Like the poet Gerard Manley Hopkins once wrote and my Uncle

Nip often reasserted, "the dearest freshness deep down in things" is still there, at least where they have not been destroyed, but civilized man is unable to sense it, his "foot being shod."

And slowly civilized man loses the very nature of who he is. He loses himself. The possibility that he can rediscover his own primal self becomes less and less likely. And though at one moment he may still be able to sense the rage of a mother bear defending her cubs, or sometime become so terrified by something that goes bump in the night that he is unable to move, these will be but brief encounters with his primal past. They will only remind civilized man of something in himself he wants to disavow, unless he can create a scholarship of anthropology out of it, and begin to study primal man with the belief that he has the key to civilization's present-day predicament. And perhaps he does, for civilized man questions the origins and ways of primal peoples as if their way of life is a mystery that must be solved or views their creation accounts as merely myths that can be explained. Civilized man must search for answers and affirmations or he is doomed.

But what else can he do? His only reality is the artificial world he's created. To act on the feelings generated by those poets who remind him of a forgotten past, he must remove the artificial reality, but he cannot do that because it has become his only reality. Yet he cannot adapt to that civilized world he and those like him have created. He cannot adapt like his ancestors did to the natural world. He cannot adapt to himself. And he will never know the spiritual peace that comes from the most fundamental primal belief: that which the children of the Earth do not comprehend as they travel the roads of the Earth and which becomes clear to them only when they have passed on into the great mysteries in Wah-kon-tah.

For the concept of Wah-kon-tah is the essence of primal thought and achievement. It is that sharing togetherness of all things. It is that interconnectedness of all things living together. It is that incomprehensible totality that always was, without beginning and without end.

From the concept of Wah-kon-tah, the primal mind associates all forms of life as being equally important. In a universe that is unimaginable in breadth and diversity, it is a fitting thought. Such an abstract concept as the Great Holy Mystery enables primal man to regard the earth as a living cosmic entity, one that must be female as she is the bearer of life. It is only logical then that the female power is acknowledged and that women are regarded as sacred beings. Though there are isolated exceptions, patriarchal societies seem unnatural to most of those who live in a primal state of mind. We are children of the earth; we have always thrived in matrilineal societies.

Civilized man, however, created a supreme being in his own male likeness. The Catholic Church has even officially decreed — just a few years ago — that God is male. Civilized man exists in male-dominated, patrilineal societies, living out his days unconsciously trying to fill the void he has created between himself and the natural world. He lives in a spiritual paradox of discontent and unhappiness. He lives out his days trying to avoid or destroy the concept of Wah-kon-tah, and that is his ultimate loss.

Thus, civilized man does indeed seem a curious creature to the primitive man who, as Uncle Nip had said, would not wantonly trade places with him because that loss would be too great.

Where and when we humans separated in our thought processes may be expressed in the words of a story that a primal mind weaves around an open fire upon returning from a prayer-fast, or it may be a scientist's theory, created with the help of an electron microscope. Yet it's a reality that this division in our thinking has occurred, and that civilizations have, indeed, spread like cancers on the earth. And soon it will become a stark reality to students of Native American literature, and to many others as well, that we do, in fact, need to return to some semblance of the spirituality and the wisdom of primal thought if we, as a species, are to evolve and continue on the earth as we know her.

An important part of my life's purpose is to remember and to cling to as much of the primal mind as I can. A new epoch may perhaps be dawning as more and more of the civilized thinkers come to value, respect, and cherish the primal thinkers, and everything they represent: love of the earth, peaceful coexistence with nature, sacred respect for all of creation.

Maybe the world needs a new manifesto, one that remembers an old vision:

The Primal Manifesto

It is time for the civilized mind to respect and learn from the primal mind, time to reconnect with our common primal roots.

It is time to respect the Earth, in all ways, to acknowledge our interrelatedness with all life forms.

It is time to allow all indigenous people to choose their way of life, and leave them alone on their own lands, if that is their choice.

It is time to respect the religious and cultural traditions of all primal people.

It is time to stop the violence inflicted against the Earth and Sky.

It is time to stop killing animals for any reason other than necessity.

It is time to stop all profit-motivated exploitation of our cetacean, four-legged, and winged relatives under the guise of education or for the sake of entertainment.

It is time to stop violence toward other people, time to support those in need.

It is time to honor women and to make decisions based on the welfare of future generations.

It is time to celebrate a diverse universe, to remember we share a common heritage, and are all related, regardless of race, religion, or choices of lifestyle.

It is time to love our Mother Earth and our Father, the Sky.

It is time to acknowledge our sacred relationship to the power of the mighty Sun.

It is time to remember that we are all an integral part of the Wheel of Life, and the Great Holy Mystery.

It is time.

CHAPTER 2

Original Instruction

*In understanding the role of peace in the Fifth World,
on which we are now embarking, we must first seek
inner-peace.... In the modern world where the serene
forests are not always available, confusion, worry,
hurry, and noise take their toll.... Peace lives in the
hearts and minds of those who seek the silent places of
the spirit....*

— Jamie Sams
The Sacred Path

Draped over the sliding glass doors, serving as a
kind of curtain for the American Indian Movement Survival School, Heart of the Earth, was a tattered
American flag. It hung upside-down against the glass,
shielding our eyes from the stone image of a crucified
Christ that hung on the wall of the Catholic church
across the street and from the old, sick elms that lined
the sidewalks on either side.

All American flags displayed in the Minneapolis American Indian housing projects back in 1974 hung upside-down. Like the old and dying elms, they were symbols of a collective awareness — something William Butler Yeats called Spiritus Mundi. It was in the spirit of that collective awareness that we chose to hang the flag that way — as an international signal for a nation in distress. And it was that Spiritus Mundi that made such a blatant display as the upside-down American flag an act of pure defiance. It symbolized a way of life that refused to die.

On the wall opposite the flag, I had hung a poster. The words I had written on it were bold and black:

**IF WE DO NOT SURVIVE AS A PEOPLE FOLLOW-
ING THE INSTRUCTION AND PURPOSE OF OUR
CREATION, THEN WE MUST ASK OURSELVES:
WHAT IS THE PURPOSE OF OUR SURVIVAL?**

These words guided the foundation of the small AIM school, and represented one of the first ideas that the young American Indian students were exposed to. For many of them, kindergarten through twelfth grade, were exiles from the Minneapolis public schools, trying to return to their heritage. Since I and the other teachers, Indian and white, had taught reading and writing and every other subject offered through the literature, history, and philosophy of Native America, it was an appropriate concept to begin to understand. You could say that it served as the first stimulus for that original seed of knowledge recorded in their ancestral DNA.

I had copied the words about our Original Instruction from a back issue of an *Akwesasne Notes* newspaper. At that time, *Akwesasne Notes* was a sort of seasonal Indian manifesto. It provided us a rare traditional perspective of what was happening to the native people and their lands all over the Western hemisphere via the tiny Mohawk reservation Akwesasne, Land Where the Partridge Drums, located within the boundaries of upstate New York where the paper was conceived.

I recall that the words I had selected for the poster came from an issue of the Notes that pictured on the front page an Indian family hanging upside-down from the branch of a rubber tree somewhere in the Amazon region of Brazil. Alongside them stood two bearded white men. Perhaps it was for these white men a moment of their civilized collective awareness — their kind of Spiritus Mundi when the symbolism of an expressed act or a displayed object goes beyond its obvious meanings and reaches even further into the collective unconscious of a civilized nation in a different kind of distress.

While one of the men posed leaning on his rifle, the other pressed one hand against the rubber tree, holding a six-gun by his side. The Indian people hanging upside-down were all dead. They appeared to be a man, two women, one who was elderly, and a child. The man and woman were probably husband and wife. The child seemed to be around eleven or twelve years old, about the age of my son Carises.

The words I had copied from that edition of the *Notes* and had placed on the poster at the tiny AIM school in Minneapolis back in 1974 mirrored the great truths of our struggle to remain Indians in a world now dominated by people who, in their rush to become civilized and superior, have turned the whole world upside-down. For they are the ones who have lost touch with their Original Instruction and have simply forgotten how to remain human.

Twenty-five years after I'd hung that poster on the AIM survival school wall, in the middle of a Florida summer and the beginning of my forty-seventh year, the challenge to live according to the poster's philosophy was never greater. I had just been offered a permanent full-time faculty position at the college where I'd been teaching only a few classes a semester. The rest of the time I used for writing. It was a fine lifestyle. It was one of the most creative periods of my life. But problems arose, as expected for any artist in a civilized world. Some of them were natural and expected. Others were threatening and unexpected. We were living on only what my wife Simone earned working part-time at the local library and on my meager adjunct paycheck every six weeks. Though our children never did without what was needed to make them happy, they were growing faster than Simone or I could have imagined — "like Florida weeds," Uncle Nip would say. They were eating more and needing more.

And though I became a prolific writer during this time, I could see only two choices before me: to take the full-time faculty position the college offered, or to take Simone and the children and cut our ties to the civilized world, for I had experienced enough human ignorance, and I found myself becoming less tolerant of civilized behavior, a behavior that violated the earth that I still loved and called Mother.

Something else happened that added fuel to my hostile emotional state: the Internal Revenue Service suddenly took an interest in me. This frightened Simone. She believed that the Feds had conspired against us, for the first IRS letter came only a week after I gave a political lecture that focused on imprisoned AIM leader Leonard Peltier. My presentation took place at the Friends of the Quakers Meeting House in St. Petersburg before a gathering of about a hundred Quakers and other interested people.

I felt like the civilized world was closing in on me. I couldn't see the beauty in the world anymore. I could be watching a sunset on the Gulf of Mexico, but my attention wouldn't be on the colors of the sky or the light dancing on the water, but on the man-made obstacles disrupting it: the telephone wires, the power boats, the condos.

I was a man who was losing touch with beauty. Even the air felt more polluted, and the Gulf waters that had always nurtured me now carried more "red tide" than I could ever remember. Television newscasters called it a "natural phenomenon." They told us that nature controls fish populations by producing the red tide.

I couldn't accept that. I believe its origin can be

traced to a technologically crazed and irresponsible civilization that has somehow helped to cause billions of deadly microscopic organisms to thrive in the warm summer waters of the Gulf of Mexico. They reproduce at such an alarming rate that they become, along with over-fishing by humans, yet another deadly part of the great imbalance that exists in the oceans of our world. During a red-tide outbreak, all kinds of sea life absorb the tiny organisms and die by the tens of thousands. Had the red tide been a natural phenomenon that had always occurred, as industrial scientists and the local chamber of commerce would have us believe, I'm sure the indigenous people of the Gulf Coast would have accounted for such a catastrophic event in their stories and songs. After all, such a disaster occurring even once would have horrified the primal mind. Yet, to my knowledge, there is not one song, not one reference to such a disaster in all Native American oral tradition.

My wife, our children, and I can never erase from our living memories what we saw that summer when death burned the air, for the beach that had always filled us with refreshing salty breezes instead was making us gasp and cough. We found ourselves having to hold our breath against the stench of all the dead and dying sea life scattered along the shoreline.

All this made me wonder if we really could survive following our Original Instruction in such an industrial and polluted world. Could we maintain the primal perspective necessary for our survival as a people, or would we, like so many before us, be sacrificed to the money god and to the "culture of consumption"?

We couldn't consider moving to a reservation. Our ideas were politically too potent. We knew from past experiences that we would more than likely: be considered outside agitators. We could be the spark that lights the fuse of the political powder keg that exists on many reservations.

Where could we go? Or was leaving it all behind the answer — and was there a place on Earth where a man and his family could live away from the influences of civilized men? I imagined a frozen Inuit village with oil wells pumping around government tract housing and a Christian church intruding on the arctic landscape. With my mind's eye I could travel to the other end of this hemisphere and see Yanomani men, women, and children lying on the floor of the rain forest in South America all bloody and dead from wounds inflicted by the guns of civilized, gold-crazed, and cattle-ranching interlopers.

Civilized men — they were everywhere. There was no escape for me. Besides, there were other things to consider. Would I be asking too much of my family? The only home our children had really known was where we lived now. And what about the other insidious cancer that grew inside the body of my wife? I had to regard all of this, for Uncle Nip taught me how a primal mind considers the effects of his decisions and actions on his whole world, not only on himself.

Then, of course, I needed to consider my vision, the one I received when I was a young teacher at Heart of the Earth. How could I fulfill my responsibility to it?

For several days and nights I contemplated what to do. I meditated. I read. I prayed, holding the pipe close to my heart, that I would make the right decision for me, for my family, and for the Earth. It was consoling to discover that I wasn't the only one ever faced with such a decision. In my readings I was reminded of all the Native people who tried to flee the white man's civilization. And I was reminded of those remote places on the Earth now invaded by the cancers of industrial technology. I was reminded of other men, like Henry David Thoreau, whose decision over a century ago to leave the solitude of Walden changed the course of human history.

Though I figured that I may never write an essay to compare with "Civil Disobedience," I could still, nevertheless, reflect on Thoreau's reasoning for leaving Walden, for I, too, felt an obligation to serve the Earth and to contribute something of myself to the welfare of the planet and my species.

And I found myself grappling with these questions: How civilized am I? How primal am I? Can the primal mind survive at all in the civilized world? Can the civilized mind learn anything of value from the primal?

Except for pockets around the earth — sacred places where indigenous people live in the Old Way, places we should fight to preserve — we cannot live completely disconnected from civilization.

I'm here to try to live within a civilization, within an ocean of civilized minds, and to try to retain all the beauty I can of my primal mind, and try to teach as much as I can about it. My life has evolved into an experiment in which I attempt to retain as much of the primal as I possibly can in a civilized world.

And so, that summer of my forty-seventh year, my life would imitate the serpent leaving his skin, shedding the old, growing into the new, all the while staying close to the Earth. And I would gain greater insight into those words regarding our Original Instruction — words about purpose, words rooted in our creation, words that allow the human being an identity beyond the illusion of civilization.

As the moon waxed and waned and time raced by, I would occasionally glimpse an insight into the meaning of the concept of our Original Instruction, like the day I was praying for a hopeful sign that would help me to see that I would grow toward a promising future from past experiences. Circles rose from the pipe bowl as I smoked — one after another after another, connecting the sacred hoop of family to what was to what would soon be, intertwining the past, present, and future, reminding me that there is no beginning nor end to the Mystery that rules the universe.

Other times an insight about our Original Instruction would drift into my mind on soft tropical breezes, bringing me closer to the awareness that we are, indeed, part of an incomprehensible totality that always was and will always be. Or it would come into my dreams just before waking. But soon the insights would no longer emanate solely from my actions and state of mind, nor from the memories of those profound printed words that I'd hung on an AIM survival school wall, nor from the haunting black and white image I'd seen on the cover of a Native American newspaper. They would come from dolphins.

A friend of ours, who once worked as a volunteer at the Dolphin Research Center (DRC) and who had recently read my book *Native Heart*, made arrangements for me, Simone, and our youngest son, Carises, to visit with the dolphins on Grassy Key, a small island in the middle of the Florida Keys, connected to the mainland only by the long bridges and the narrow road of Highway 1.

Carises and I had been told that special arrangements were made for us to swim with dolphins. The possibility of visiting and swimming with captive dolphins, however, made me uncomfortable, for the idea of tearing a dolphin from the Wheel of Life for any reason that centered around humans had enraged me since I was a boy. Our friend, however, had reassured me several times that these dolphins were not captive in the sense that I had suspected and feared.

Most of the twelve dolphins that we were to visit at DRC had been retired from amusement parks where they had withdrawn, refusing to perform for their "trainers," or they had become too weak and sick to entertain the public. A few had resisted any contact with humans and turned violent. The business administrators and promoters of some of the private and public aquariums all over North America chose to ship the dejected dolphins to DRC. They did this rather than bear the burden of publicly explaining an attack on a human by a dolphin in one of their amusement parks, or the death of a dolphin in one of their concrete-and-glass enclosed tanks.

Not all the dolphins who lived at DRC, however, came from such notorious backgrounds. Two of them were born there. One was named Tursi. She is the daughter of Flipper, the famous dolphin who starred in the TV show named after him. I regard Flipper as the first dolphin ambassador to civilized humans of this century.

There was another dolphin, though, with a much sadder story who came to live at DRC. I was told that she, like the others, had been snatched from the ocean when she was young, about five years old, just about the time she would have chosen a mate. Instead of fulfilling her purpose within the dolphin's code of their Original Instruction and living a life that the Great Holy Mystery had intended for her kind, she was stolen from her pod and sold to the U.S. Navy. For twenty-five years Josephine had been used for "physical research." What kind of "physical research" was done to her no one at DRC was told, and none of the sailors and others who brought her there offered any more information.

The story we heard was that Josephine had unexpectedly outlived her worth to the Navy scientists, that she had resisted further contact with humans, and that it seemed as though she would soon die, so the Navy had prepared to do away with her. Had it not been for the sailors from the base where she'd been captive all those years, she would probably not be alive today. And that would have been a great loss.

The sailors, who had learned of the dolphin's condition, raised enough of their own money to pay for a military transport to fly her down to the small airport on Marathon Island where she was met by the folks at DRC, and then taken in a Ryder's rental truck on the short drive to Grassy Key. The idea of sailors doing this for a dolphin puzzled me. But I was to learn soon enough that dolphins can do that to a civilized man whose spirit hasn't completely disappeared. Dolphins can make humans act out of character — make them remember their humanness and their connection to their Original Instruction.

Josephine's story was just one of several I'd heard about the dolphins at DRC; so, under pressure from Carises, who saw this visit and opportunity to swim with dolphins as the chance of a lifetime, and for Simone, who had recently been told by a surgeon that she had breast cancer, I yielded, and we headed south from St. Petersburg. Together we rode in our old black Mustang on I-275, over the great expanse of the Skyway Bridge and the gleaming turquoise sea where the Gulf of Mexico flows into Tampa Bay, toward Sarasota, and eventually on to Naples. Then we turned east on Alligator Alley and headed into the Everglades.

Perhaps it was while traveling through the glades and passing places like Shark Island that I realized how a man can suddenly feel drawn to a particular place, a place that connects him to something old, a place he will knowingly "give himself up to." It was as if destiny was taking us down to Grassy Key to be with the dolphins, and while driving through the glades I felt some other kind of collective unconscious drawing us there, a Spiritus Mundi that intertwined us with other life forms. And as we traveled on, I couldn't help but become better aware of the beauty that is the "grassy river" called the Everglades.

Everything I'd been told about it was true. There really is nothing on Earth that reflects such delicate balance and rare beauty as the Florida Everglades. That's not simply echoing the sentiment of environmental slogans used to rally human support to protect this watery world from the hands of farmers, ranchers, industrialists, and developers. It's much more than that. Perhaps the centenarian, Marjorie Stoneman Douglas, described the uniqueness of the Everglades as well as anyone. In her 1947 book, *River of Grass*, she captures in words the awesome beauty of this incredible place:

> The water moves. The sawgrass, pale green to deep-brown ripeness, stands rigid. It is moved only in sluggish rollings by the vast push of the winds across it. Over its endless acres here and there the shadows of the dazzling clouds quicken and slide, purple-brown, plum-brown, mauve-brown, rust-brown, bronze. The bristling, blossoming tops do not bend easily like stands of grain. They do not even, in their own growth, curve all one way but stand in edge clumps, curving against

each other, all the massed curving blades making millions of fine arching lines that in a little distance merge to a huge expanse of brown wires, or bristles or, farther beyond, to deep-piled plush. At the horizon they become velvet. The line they make is an edge of velvet against the infinite blue, the blue-and-white, the clear, fine primrose yellow, the burning brass and crimson, the molten silver, the deepening hyacinth sky. . . .

Truly, no place exists on the Earth like the Everglades. We traveled through it as if the three of us were moving through primordial time together. It was as if we were each leaving behind something of our civilized selves, something of our last lingering civilized way of seeing life, and we were heading toward something else, something new and unimaginable — something that both excited and frightened us. It was as if I were recalling the feelings I had waking up from dolphin dreams — recent dreams that I couldn't remember except for the feelings that remained long after I had awakened. It felt as if we were each being summoned there, perhaps to participate in our own evolutionary process, or even that of our species.

We were returning to what we once were.

But even though the anticipation of meeting the dolphins at DRC was growing inside of me, I still couldn't escape the idea of dolphins, captive and broken, diluted of spirit, deprived of their purpose, and denied the essence of their own Original Instruction by arrogant humans who have made it their primary function in life to make money. Whether it's the Japanese fishermen who slaughter dolphins because the dolphins eat the same fish that make the fishermen profit, or whether it's humans who net dolphins for money, snatching them from the pods of their Original Instruction to sell to other humans who make more money by putting them on display for entertainment, they're all civilized humans who regard themselves as the superior beings of this Earth.

So, what would I discover at DRC that would be different? What would I bear witness to?

Thoughts like these settled in my mind when we arrived on Grassy Key and pulled off Highway 1 and onto the sand and gravel of a little place decorated with old wooden crab traps and strands of colored Christmas lights. A sign with the name Bonefish painted on it hung near the road.

As we rolled to a stop near the main house, we paused in the car, gazing at the ocean in front of us. I imagined that Simone and Carises were thinking the same thing I was because each of us got out of the car and stood for a moment taking it all in. On each side of the sand- and shell-paved driveway stood several small cottages located right on the shore of the Atlantic. They were operated by two retired nurses who, like a lot of people living in the Keys, had exited a big northern city, seeking to escape the stress of civilization, materialism, and overpopulation. They too flew south, just about as far south as one can go and still be in the same country.

We rented a nice little old trailer-type house there. It

had a pine deck, and long green fronds of huge coconut palms swayed over it. They served as a natural canopy, shielding us against the searing heat of the tropical sun. While leaning on the wooden railing and standing under this sweeping canopy, we stared in awe at the turquoise Atlantic. No sight in the world could be more beautiful. We could feel the energy emanating from such beauty. I was hoping that this could be a healing place for Simone — a place where the natural beauty would help her mind to restore her self-image and make her body well again, a place where the rampant cells of cancer, much like the civilized cells of the modern cities we had left behind, are overwhelmed by the power and the splendor of the natural world. I hoped her cancer would be absorbed by that which makes things beautiful and beneficial for the body again, and restores balance back to the body again.

Around an hour or so before sunset on the first day at Bonefish, Carises and I took a canoe out into the clear water of the Atlantic and headed along the southern shore of Grassy Key, under the bridge of Highway 1, to the Gulf side, and to the Dolphin Research Center. Along the way we passed over live coral and crabs and fish the likes of which we'd never seen except in books.

We were in paradise, or what was left of paradise before the intrusion of civilized man. We passed under and through mangroves and around estuaries of snowy egrets, cormorants, herons, and ibis, though we couldn't help but notice the pollution that these self-proclaimed superior beings of civilization had created from the resources of this land: the numbers of discarded aluminum Bud Light and Coors beer cans, of the soda cans of the Coke and Pepsi generation still shining on the sandy bottom, the old Goodyear car and truck tires we would occasionally see half-buried in the sea grass, the plastic diapers and black plastic trash bags that swayed in the undercurrents, or the clear plastic six-pack wrappers that floated by.

There were lots of flip tops, Carises noted. And cigarette butts. One of the people at DRC would tell us a few days later that a beached sea turtle they had tried to save had recently died. The autopsy revealed that the turtle's stomach was blocked with some 300 cigarette butts. She'd mistaken them for food — cigarette butts that the "superior beings" from a civilized world had conveniently tossed over the sides of their boats or had thrown out the windows of their cars.

It was nearly dark when Carises and I returned. Simone sat reading on the shore. Her long black hair and brown skin in the shadows of twilight under the palms brought me back in time. It was the same feeling I had traveling through the glades, when time is of the Mystery and reality becomes transcendent. The image of Simone on the shore at Bonefish could have been a scene recorded in some Spaniard's journal, when he first described the splendor of this land and water, and the

grace and beauty of the "Indios." What startled me was
how she appeared more like a ghost out of the future,
not one from the past. I paddled harder toward her.

As we sat together on the dock, I held her in my
arms. We talked about how the beauty of Grassy Key
endures in defiance of the cancer of Western civilization. I told her about the human waste Carises and I had
seen along the way. Then I said that Simone's beauty is
like that of this island's, strong and enduring, and inside
I could feel myself hoping to make it so. Finally, I settled
down and told her what she had assured me from the
beginning, that the dolphins at DRC were actually in
the Gulf of Mexico and not in artificial tanks, that the
only thing separating them from total freedom was a
two-to-three-foot fence. I said that it seemed they could
easily jump over it if they wanted to, especially at high
tide when the fence was only about a foot above the
water's surface. I told her about the two dolphins that
emerged on either side of our canoe:

"The water was as still as the air. It was nearly
sunset. I could see Carises at the bow end with his
paddle on his knees. He would glance back to me then
to the dolphins. I looked at him. I think that we were
both acknowledging their size. Their big fins. Their penetrating eyes. The sounds of their breathing. Their
bodies seemed as long as the canoe. And even though
they were dolphins, it was apparent that if they had
wanted to, they could've tossed us from the canoe and
torn us to shreds. We were in their world, I knew, but
we understood this, which is why I thought we'd be

safe." Then I laughed, "At any time during the en-counter, Carises and I may have reconsidered the idea of swimming the next day with their relatives. They seemed that big to us, Simone. They seemed that pow-erful."

I described to her how other dolphins came to regard us, and somehow seemed to even measure our intentions. They were the ones behind the fence, the ones who lived at DRC. They too rose eye-level out of the water and looked at us.

"Simone, sometimes it felt as though the dolphins were reading us. Other times it felt as though we were being told something telepathically." And I told her how I'd been wondering about the silent language of the dol-phins, for it seemed as though in some way I'd been lis-tening to it all my life. At that moment the idea of dolphins communicating with us in this way seemed so real to me. Maybe the reason was that I was older now, more conscious of the unexplainable than I used to be. Or maybe it was simply that I became aware of that primal part of me, the part where childhood innocence allows a man to trust what his heart knows and under-stands.

All the time that Carises and I remained in the canoe, silent and still, the two dolphins remained with us, one on each side of us, with their eyes just above the water's surface.

Later that evening, when the island seemed so peaceful and quiet, I joined my wife and son on the shore at Bonefish, and we laid underneath the southern night sky and the vast expanse of stars.

In the Florida Keys the stars can shine like no place I've ever seen. On warm nights after a thunderstorm has passed, leaving the air clean and clear, stars appear everywhere — unimaginable numbers of them in an incomprehensible black ocean of sea and space that stretches from horizon to horizon and beyond. You look at the sky and you see endless stars; you look at the water and you see endless reflections of stars.

Carises recalled Indian legends about them. "Coyote must've been carrying a big bag of rocks when he fell," he said. Carises wondered which star might be Grandma's campfire, the one she traveled to when she died.

Simone likened the sight to some nights she'd seen while camping in the boundary waters of northern Minnesota. Only here in the Keys there was no buzzing from pesky summer mosquitoes or chilling cold from northern winds. We heard only the occasional splashes of mullet and other fish, and felt the balmy Atlantic breeze . . . and saw the endless stars!

Then, in the time it takes for a single star to fall across the sky, it felt as though a thought that had been planted in my head weeks ago suddenly sprouted. Perhaps it was one of the reasons I felt drawn to this place. At that moment I acknowledged my unconditional love for Simone. I would not cower in the face of my wife's cancer. I would stay by her side no matter what, even if it meant that we would have to live with the idea of cancer being a part of our lives one more year or eighty more years.

"I love you," I whispered to her. "I adore you...."
And I would love and adore her even more now.

And while our youngest child remained zoned on the stars, I held my wife's hand, and we talked into the night about the experience that Carises and I had that day with the dolphins. I told Simone that I was relieved that the dolphins' existence wasn't limited to an aquarium, but that my concern now was seeing them denied a meaningful life — a life that would still allow them purpose.

As we shared and exchanged ideas, our bitterness for humans who abuse the rights of dolphins rose to the surface. Neither Simone nor I had any tolerance for people who steal the freedom of other species and use them as a source of entertainment and profit, and then disguise this "big business" as a way to "educate" humans — humans too confined by their civilized minds and artificial extensions to experience dolphins in the wild when the dolphins choose to, or humans too arrogant or removed from themselves to seek the dolphin wisdom through the agent of a dream. "If I go to DRC tomorrow feeling pity for the way they live, the dolphins will pick up on that, Simone. I don't want to remind them that their spirits have been broken. I don't want to help make them more aware of how their life purpose has been cut short and destroyed. The last thing I want them to feel is pity from me."

As a layer of clouds spread over the night sky like a billowy blanket, the three of us returned to our own covers of cotton sheets in our little cottage under the swaying coconut palms. We went to sleep as tropical breezes rattled the leaves of the fronds and drifted into our minds. In the warmth of soft winds, a special dream came that would forever alter the way I saw the world and the way I saw the dolphins at DRC. The dream brought me closer to understanding the meaning of the words regarding our Original Instruction, those black printed words that once hung on the wall of a small Indian school, words that I can still see when I close my eyes.

In my dream that night I saw dolphins all around me. They spoke to me in the silent language that conveys thoughts without sound. They were of one mind and heart. They spoke to me as one voice.

"We have chosen this existence at this time in our lives as you have chosen yours. We are captive as you are captive, but that is the choice we have made. Like you, it is a choice that allows our lives a sense of purpose. It is doubtful that we can survive anymore like our ancestors had, so it is with you. Perhaps someday returning to that way of life will come to pass. For now, though, we choose to remain here as teachers; as you have chosen, so have we."

When I awoke from the dream, the sun was just coming up. I watched from the railing of the pine deck. Simone and Carises joined me. The sun was rising right out of the ocean — a sight I had seldom seen, and one that Carises and Simone never had. We had always lived on the Gulf coast of Florida, where we often watch the sunset as a ritual. Until now we had never stood together on the shore and seen it rise in this way. But this was Grassy Key, and the shore where we were standing was facing the Atlantic — southeast, the direction where the light of understanding and rebirth shines. The sky was a wash of pastel pink and bluejay down.

Over orange juice and toast, we sat around the small table on the pine deck of our cottage, and I recounted my dream to Simone and Carises, recalling, as closely as I could, what the dolphins had told me. I was anxious now to meet them. Just hours ago I was uncomfortable, uncertain of my attitude and how it would affect them. I didn't want to offend them. I was sure that they had been offended enough in their lives. I knew that they had experienced enough of human attitudes and exploitation, and that they didn't need me to bring along my bag of pity by reminding them of the lives they'd been denied.

To some extent I understood part of what they experienced and felt because I was trying to live my life as a primal-thinking, contemporary Indian, living in what the American expatriate poet, e.e. cummings, described as "a world of unborn." I too was torn from the Wheel when I was young and trained to be something I wasn't. I too resisted and was considered dangerous and embarrassing. I too found purpose and self-worth in spite of this. My Indian relatives believed the dolphins had chosen me to help interpret their needs. I had taken their words to heart, aware of the responsibilities that go with them, for that morning before first light I had received a dream, and as the sun slowly rose in the horizon of sea and sky, I understood that this was going to be a day like no other in my life. On this day I would become a student teacher once again, only this time I would observe teachers of another species, and the classroom where I'd make my observations would be in the warm waters of the Gulf of Mexico.

Though the sun hadn't reached above the tops of the pines and palms, the energy that stirs with its appearance was already present at DRC when we pulled off the sandy trail along Highway 1 and onto the shell and gravel parking lot of DRC. The energy was all around us. It washed over us.

The people we met inside the pavilion were smiling and friendly. Laurel, our special guide and DRC's photographer, introduced herself and offered to escort us down toward the shore and to the dolphins. On the cool, sandy, shell-white trails, and under the shade of slash pines and coconut palms, we walked toward the sounds of life coming from the Gulf water just ahead. Peacocks strutted casually across our path, and parrots of all kinds and colors squawked at the arrival of people and the sun, which by now had peaked over the tree line and was beaming down on the silvery gray beings moving through the dark green water at the edge of the trail.

First, there were the strong and deep sounds of their

breathing, and then powerful sprays of air burst from the water's surface, that beckoned and lured us toward them. The life-breath sounds made each of us more aware of the dolphins' connection and relationship to us. Then they came toward us, three of them. They rose slightly out of the water....

It must be their eyes that lock on to you and the way they seem to look into you that makes you conscious of something outside yourself, something that makes you an equal in the Circle of Life, no more or less important than anything else. It's something that can humble some of us and frighten or anger others. It's the idea of being in the presence of beings whose intelligence expands our human imagination....

The sounds of their life-breath filled the air. Then there were sharp whistles, quickly followed by rapid clicking sounds — like some kind of code that called us closer to the water. Then we sensed a silent penetration of our minds, as if they were learning something about our deeper selves, something that reveals our true nature and character.

Simone remained on shore while Carises and I entered the warm water. She would still cough occasionally from a long bout with a summer cold, and she refused to carry any sickness to the dolphins. Memories of the diseases of civilization — smallpox, the coughing sickness, measles, mumps, and the anguish of the Ojibway midé priests as they fought against mass death would allow her no other choice. And so, she watched the transformation of her son and her husband and was part of the experience by observing from the shore.

For me, the descent into the water that day would be like reliving another dream that I'd had, this one more than a year earlier, when an elderly dolphin questioned me about human behavior. "Why are humans so different?" he asked. "Why can some of you hate and kill us without regard, and why are there even more of you who care nothing about the world of the dolphin?

"And yet, why are there humans, like your family, who love us and respect the blessings and the balance of life, and care for our world?

"What makes you so different?"

I explained that it was our beliefs that made humans so different, and the moment I said this, I realized I was understanding something about my own past and my own identity: how "Indianness" really isn't something measured by a percentage of blood, defined by a government, or claimed through an enrollment number — being Indian is more a way of looking at and living in this world.

"You are our elder and wiser relatives," I said.

And then I reflected that a major purpose for many of the old stories and legends is to make us better aware of our primal dependency on other life forms — aware of how other life forms provide sustenance as well as basic ways to live in harmony with our environment. Children of the earth, like the dolphins, for instance, have been living much longer than humans have, and the dolphin journey on the river of Time and Knowing has provided their species a world of countless lifetime experiences. From these experiences the dolphins and other related cetaceans have evolved into a spiritual state of existence. Such longevity has allowed the dolphins and their cousins to luxuriate and appreciate life in all its simplicity and splendor.

I told the elder dolphin in my dream that night that we all shared the breath of life. "Some of us have beliefs that don't allow us to see ourselves as superior creatures," I said.

As I stood there at DRC about to meet the dolphins, I also recollected what I'd learned about the web of life. And I could hear the challenges of my Uncle Nip: "How can the people of any species be superior if all things are interrelated in a Totality and dwell in a Universe that is incomprehensible?"

I closed my eyes and saw, as if in a dream, my uncle in his kitchen stirring the contents of a saucepan and glancing up at me. "Only in his civilized-thinking mind is he superior." He turned to me with a twinkle in his sky blue eyes. "I assure you, Nephew," he said smiling, "humans are not the pinnacle of creation."

In the water you can feel the dolphins see into you. It's as though they scan you. It is as if our life-essence has recorded the energies of our life experiences and revealed our intentions. The dolphins scanned this essence as if they were scanning the books of our lives to determine who Carises and I really were.

That's what it felt like when we were in the water with them. And when Tursi and her son Talon leaned into me as I swam and offered their dorsal fins, I did as I was instructed by the facilitators at the center, and gently took hold of each dorsal like I would a child's arm. Even as they pulled me faster and faster, my grip never endangered their dorsals. I was conscious and certain of that while I rode alongside them.

Three more dolphins, one with her baby, joined us and moved through the water near me. The collective energy of the pod was exhilarating. I hadn't felt such a collective sense of power since one of the first AIM powwows to honor the Earth. The dolphins maneuvered like graceful dancers and moved through the water with great speed. They did this without depending on artificial extensions and without endangering their environment or creating havoc among the other life forms that share the sea with them. Such innate strength cracks that psychological wall of assumed civilized superiority.

As I felt the self-generating power of the pod, I also felt my vulnerability. I knew for certain that Tursi and her son Talon could ride me right through those mangroves, over that fence, and out into the Gulf if they had a mind to. Yet I believe there wasn't a happier and more trusting man on the earth that day. For a man or woman to rediscover the forgotten child inside each of them is to rediscover a sense of trust in the universe. And while swimming in a pod of dolphin teachers, I began to recapture the awe that comes from wonder and the joy that comes from innocence. While riding in a dolphin pod I learned to trust openly and whole-heartedly the universe.

That afternoon after our morning swim, I stood out front of the DRC pavilion, watching a family. The man was tall, balding, and middle-aged. Alongside him, but at a short distance, stood a thin, short woman with red hair cropped just above her shoulders, and a small, pale ten year old. They had just stepped out of a white Mercedes Benz with gold trim. It was the same Mercedes that a truck had side-swiped the night before — we had heard the squealing tires and crunching crash of metal against metal.

The previous night, Simone and I had seen the result of another violent encounter of civilized minds in artificial extensions. From what we could tell, it appeared that the man was backing his Mercedes out of one of the expensive hotels on Grassy Key. Because he had pulled in from the wrong direction, he was hit by a pickup whizzing by with a bright red, white, and blue Kawasaki jet ski riding in the truck's bed.

Though no one was hurt, the crash left the Mercedes with a twisted bumper and a broken taillight. The man who owned the car stood at the rear-end assessing the damage. We watched him snap his arm in the direction of the motel where he and his family were staying, and without raising his voice or any other visible sign of emotion, he told his wife and son to go back to the room.

Their car costs more than our house, I thought, and I wondered how they could have so much material wealth, yet still appear so unhappy. I wondered if that wasn't the ultimate sacrifice many people pay for expensive cars and extravagant homes. The man checked his gold watch and reexamined his car in the DRC parking lot that morning. His wife and son stood nearby. Even as they headed for the entrance of DRC, they appeared as isolated from each other as they were from their environment. I had imagined that DRC was probably on their list of places to see and things to do on their one-week vacation from their civilized world to the Florida Keys — things to do that would help keep them busy and on schedule, too busy to take time to get reacquainted with themselves.

What they didn't expect at DRC was the absence of an artificially controlled environment. The man grumbled about the heat. I overheard the woman complaining about the humidity. The boy whined about not going to Sea World. They even shared their disdain at the idea of walking on shell and gravel in order to get inside the DRC pavilion. Isolation, disdain, and disappointment were all they seemed to share. I figured that I was observing one of the things that gives developers the ammunition they need to destroy natural environments and recreate more comfortable and convenient artificial ones instead. It was because of the technological demands of civilized people like this that our natural world was quickly falling apart.

"What are they doing here?" I muttered to Simone.

I put my arm around her, and pulled her closer. She rested her head on my chest while we followed them through the pavilion and out to where the dolphins were.

The sun's heat saturated the air and the warm water where Tursi and Talon had been cruising in wide circles. The dolphins emerged only to breathe, and the sound of their life-breath echoed among the surrounding mangroves, rocks, and trees. When Tursi slowed in front of us, we waved and greeted her in Ojibway, Simone's native language and one of the only native languages that I have retained any words from. "Anin, Tursi," I said. And Tursi stopped and rose slightly out of the water. She looked at me, observing my arm around Simone. Her polite pause and regard felt as if Tursi was exercising a tribal courtesy which teaches that the one being spoken to stops to give full attention to the one who's speaking. "Me-gwitch (thank you)," I added. "Me-gwitch for sharing yourself and your son, and for the way you left us feeling today.... You're beautiful, Tursi."

Something in the way Tursi looked at me told me she was acknowledging the intent of my words. Perhaps it was the way she tilted her head, as if she were making the effort to understand me. Or perhaps it was her dolphin smile.

When she submerged I remained on the sea wall

with Simone nestled under my arm, but my focus shifted back to the man, the woman, and the boy. They were standing on the edge of the sea wall across from where we were. They too were looking at the dolphins, but they weren't speaking, not to the dolphins, not to each other. They stood apart. Though they were a family, the distance between them was a void. They didn't smile.

I wondered if the man and woman had ever smiled, or if they had, how long ago? I wondered about the original purpose of a marriage, about the purpose of mating and perpetuating what is good about our species. I wondered if the man or woman ever even touched in a tender way, and if they'd taken enough time from their civilized existence to lovingly touch their son, that pale boy who seemed so alone standing apart from them in the bright sunlight. It didn't seem as though they had, not by the way they were standing apart from the boy, and not by the way the man was standing apart from his wife on the sea wall while Tursi and Talon swam by them, touching and caressing and luxuriating in life in the way that dolphins do.

Like when one dream shifts to another, my attention shifted from the family of humans to the family of dolphins, and I squeezed Simone closer to me and held the hand of Carises, who had joined us on the sea wall. He said that he had been looking at the incredible paintings back in the pavilion that were done by the dolphins at DRC. While the three of us watched Tursi and Talon shoot through the water to join the other dolphins, something whipped behind them in the air and into my mind. It was as though an ancient Hopi story of Spider Woman was coming to life in a contemporary, technological world.

It felt as though Spider Woman herself had sent a summer breeze, like an invisible wisp of raw cotton, to suspend this experience in time and memory. It was as though she and the dolphins had woven together an invisible web, connecting everyone who was present that afternoon at DRC to the moment. Like the pretty gem in a dream catcher that serves to attract harmful spirits, and like the strands of web that catch them before they can enter our dreams, something in the breeze at this moment, something about the joy of the dolphins on this day, prevented any negative thoughts from penetrating the web Spider Woman and the dolphins had created. I could just close my eyes and feel the goodness filter through. I wanted those tender thoughts about family and love, about peace and harmony, balance and beauty to beam through that tiny opening at the center of the web and replenish the seeds of hope I had buried deep inside.

And as those seeds were stimulated, I knew that I would never lose hope again, hope about our species, even hope for the life of Simone. No matter how small a chance there was for her survival, I would trust in that hope. I would trust in the balance of the Universe; I would trust in the Universe itself.

Rather than imposing a plan, from that point on, I would just try to relax and allow the Mystery to unfold. And while these thoughts were forming in my mind, I

could feel myself spiraling upward, toward my own evolution of understanding and maybe even inward toward
the evolution of our species. For I was tapping into that
collective unconscious that all the children of the Earth
may have shared at one time. This was a moment of illu-
mination, when the actions of dolphins created the
spark that ignited the code, and once again I realized: If
we do not survive as a people following the instruction
and purpose of our creation, then we must ask ourselves, what is the purpose of our survival?

At that moment, Tursi exploded out of the water,
flipping in the air and diving back down. Her son Talon
followed. Then another dolphin joined in. And another.
And another. Each would burst from the water, flip, and
splash back down, only to disappear and reappear. It
was as if they had stirred the energy all around us until
the energy of the air and the water and the people who
stood watching on the sea wall stirred with it too. When
I glanced up at the family who had arrived in their
dented Mercedes, I was stricken with the kind of awe
that I was to always experience profoundly around dolphins.

The tall man with hardened eyes stood on the sea
wall embracing his wife with one arm while his frail son
stood with his father's other arm resting on the boy's
shoulder. They pressed against each other as the dolphins swam past them and circled and swam past them
again and again. While the dolphins helped the spirit of
Spider Woman weave this magic, I watched as these
three humans, who had probably not smiled together in

a long time, smile broadly. The man's eyes had visibly softened. It was as though the dolphins had stimulated the code of Original Instruction inside these people. For I believe these civilized humans had felt something they couldn't define, something as old as the sun above them and as new as the seeds of promise. Hope drifted through the opening of the invisible web that Spider Woman and the dolphins had created with a wisp of summer air and the salty sea spray of visible breath.

And though the code of our Original Instruction has been suppressed over generations to the point of nonexistence among many civilized humans, it is not quite to that state in others. It is as if that part of the code originally embedded in our human DNA could still work, and is still working — a still, quiet voice of instructions coming from within. For I know that traditional Native Americans all over the Western Hemisphere are still aware of their Original Instruction. They still address the concept of the Great Holy Mystery, that incomprehensible totality of Creation that all things share, and they still show their regard for the powers and the gifts of the earth and of the sun through ceremonies and prayers.

The way of living derived from our Original Instruction is also alive on the continent of Australia among the traditional Aborigines who still walk the songlines of the ancestors in Dream Time. It is the same on the island of New Zealand among the traditional Maori, whose journey through life can mirror the gentle flight of a butterfly. And that code of living that records our Original Instruction can still be discovered in the Old Ways of the Sami, who remain standing at the edge of the Fjords in the land of the midnight sun, addressing the four quarters of the world and of the universe.

And though that part of our human DNA that retains the code of our Original Instruction has been so depleted among civilized humans, it still can exist in some distant and dormant state. As D. H. Lawrence once wrote: "Consciousness is like a web woven finely in the mind from the various silken strands spun forth from the primal center of the unconscious." Perhaps what I was experiencing while I watched these three isolated and seemingly cold-hearted and miserable human beings smile and touch one another on the sea wall at DRC was a connection to those silken strands of our human DNA that records our Original Instruction. I watched as these alienated people became a family once again.

If, in the time it takes the sun to rise from the horizon to the tree tops, they had become aware of this part of their nature, then maybe, in the way a wisp of summer air was transformed into a dream catcher that day, this one moment — this one seed of primal thought replanted or renourished by dolphins — would be promise enough to start a change in the way these civilized humans lived and how they regarded each other, and the world around them. Maybe that change would only come from their son, because he is perhaps closer to his primal existence. Maybe that change can, in some small way, help alter the destructive path that civilized man currently walks.

As I reflected on the dolphin experience at DRC days later with Simone, I understood how the dolphins had stimulated the code in those people in the way that perhaps I too can stimulate the code within the students I teach and the children I help raise, so they may be sensitive and responsible citizens of this planet, that they may understand that it is not the Original Instruction and Purpose of humans to subdue and dominate.

I told Simone that perhaps the awesome designs of the "crop circles" that we saw in the wheat fields of England stimulate the code of our Original Instruction as well. Perhaps their purpose is similar to what dolphins do to civilized people whose code hasn't completely disappeared. Maybe the intent behind the appearances and mass sightings of UFOs in the skies all over our world does the same thing. Maybe just a simple thought form of a single cell of extraterrestrial existence can serve as a catalyst for our human evolution. Maybe this is all a part of the process to stimulate the seeds of Original Instruction encoded in human DNA. I still wonder if by chance and by nurturing those seeds, they can grow. Who knows? There is more to heaven and earth — to paraphrase Hamlet — then any of us dream of.

The day after our first swim, we were invited back to DRC. That day, I saw and experienced things that even now are difficult to find words to describe. On that day DRC was closed to the public. It was the day Dr. Dave was scheduled to take severely brain-damaged children, children suffering from severe neurological disorders as well as those who were autistic, into the water to be with the dolphins — one on one. These dolphins were not captured for this purpose. It appeared to me that it was their conscious decision to stay at DRC to teach at this time and help these children. My dreams certainly contributed to this insight.

As a teacher I especially looked forward to this morning. My Uncle Nip once told me that teaching mentally disabled children was one of his first jobs after he'd completed his master's degree. By the feeling in his words and by the way his eyes smiled, I could tell that it was one of his most rewarding experiences as a teacher.

I felt very different than I had two days earlier. The depressed and morose mentality and uncomfortable feelings had disappeared. My way of looking at the world of the dolphins at DRC had been turned upside-down. Now the feelings and the insights of the dream I'd had, just before I woke up the morning of my first dolphin swim, prevailed. Now I was going to learn what the dolphins at DRC had to teach me about teaching, tolerance, and love.

The atmosphere at DRC that morning was charged when we arrived, but it was a different kind of energy than the day before. Though it seemed to originate from the same combined source — the dolphins, the sun, and the sea — the energy was unusual. It was still as strong, but more contained, more centralized, even more subtle. It was as if the wind had paused and gathered in one spot. It was as though the energy seemed more focused, and a lot of it focused on Dr. Dave.

When you first meet Dr. Dave, you have to smile. He appears sort of round and red-faced in his flowery shirt and colorful shorts. He smiled easily and friendly, and seemed pleased to discuss with me his work at DRC. His skin is freckled, fair, and vulnerable under the tropical sun, so most of the time when he's not in the water with the children and the dolphins, he's under the shade of a tree or some other shelter. Silvery gray and white hair stick out in strands from under a blue baseball cap that has a large, green rubber fish standing erect with big eyes above his forehead.

I watched as his sparkling blue eyes followed the people exiting the pavilion and heading toward the water. A fifteen-year-old boy named Kevin sat in a wheelchair being pushed by his father. Alongside them walked Kevin's mother and little brother. We had seen them the previous evening when the father had carried Kevin from the car. Kevin didn't seem to have any control over his bodily movements. His head was tucked down to his left and sort of swayed back and forth. Sometimes his mother would wipe his chin. He seemed terribly withdrawn, and terribly serious — I had a feeling he had probably never laughed, or even smiled. He was a prisoner inside his own body.

Behind him came the others. Each one rolled along in a wheelchair. A boy named Davy appeared to be in about the same condition as Kevin, only Davy was younger. He too had a face that probably had never known a smile. He too had been brought here from somewhere far away. And at the rear of the group, walking hand in hand, was a young Brazilian mother and a little boy named Lau. Lau was autistic. He was about seven years old and had never spoken a word in his life. There were others, five children in all, and the parents who brought them. Each was at DRC out of desperation and hope — the kind of hope that springs from despair.

That morning, Tursi got Kevin to extend and move his right arm from side to side. She did this while Dr. Dave stood chest deep in the water, holding Kevin in his arms. It was the first time Kevin had ever exercised this type of physical control and movement. But what must have seemed even more rewarding to the parents, who stood arm in arm on the floating dock watching, was Kevin's big smile. I imagined that they had never known their son capable of experiencing the joy that comes from that deep-down connection to life.

When Kevin's session was over, Dr. Dave picked little Davy up in his arms and carried him out to where a jetty serves as a wall to the classroom where the other dolphins were. He stepped onto a floating dock that was tied to the rocks that made up the sea wall, and he and Davy sat on the edge of it waiting for Delphi and Aphrodite to come. And they did! They leapt and flipped and twirled. First to the right of Davy, then to the left. Each time Davy would have to move his head further and further in each direction. Each time he would move it further than he'd ever moved it before. In this way Davy could follow the precise acrobatics and the huge splashes of the dolphins. His eyes beamed and his smile curved from ear to ear. The dolphins did this under no commands and without any rewards.

It was easy for me to see that they had ignited the code, not only in Davy, but the code in all of us who stood by experiencing the moment. Simone and I felt our own joy as we watched the glowing faces of Davy's family.

Later that same morning, Lau sat alone with his mom and Dr. Dave at another dock. We stood back, concealed somewhat behind a cluster of mangroves. Neither Simone nor I wanted to violate that private space around Dr. Dave, Lau, and his mom.

"Come here, Rainbow," Dr. Dave called. "Come here, Bo! Here, Bo!" And the dolphin conceived in a hurricane quickly emerged, an arm's length in front of them.

Rainbow is big, even in dolphin size. He was conceived during the "no-namer" hurricane that swept across south Florida one night shortly after the TV weathermen said it was going to rain. The storm hit after the weathermen went to bed and had blown over by morning. While most humans spent the night in terror and woke up shocked at a ripped up, watery world, the dolphins cavorted until daybreak. As a result, two rainbows were conceived: one in the morning sky, the other in a dolphin's womb.

"Bo!" called Dr. Dave again and again in his deep raspy voice. Each time he'd look at Lau and then turn and gesture with his hand toward Bo, who clicked and smiled in front of them. Suddenly, Rainbow rose most of the way into the air and shot vertically backward across the water. It was an extraordinary act. Lau stood on his tippy-toes, pointed the forefinger of his right hand and waved it in Bo's direction. "Bo!" he cried. "Bo! Bo!" It was the first articulate sound that ever came from Lau's lips. It was the first time he'd ever met a dolphin. Simone and I watched from behind the mangroves while his mother wept, and Lau remained on his toes, crying louder and louder, "Bo! Bo! Bo! Bo! Bo...."

Only the silent echo of Lau's first word was left in my mind when I found a quiet moment to sit alone under a palm-thatched roof with Dr. Dave. He greeted me with a tired smile. Sweat dripped from his forehead, down reddened freckled cheeks. Every now and again a dolphin would emerge and breathe and descend, and he would acknowledge each with a grateful and puzzling smile as they passed by. It was the kind of enigmatic smile that comes from a person who is grateful for something he doesn't truly understand.

"What do the dolphins do, Dr. Dave? How do they get the children to respond like that?"

He looked at me and said, "It's magic.... Now I know I'm a scientist, yet I can only explain it simply that way. It's magic." I realized that other animals like dogs can evoke similar feelings in humans, but the intent of the dolphins and the joy they expel seems unique to them. And because they work with such challenging situations it makes it all appear magical.

Dr. Dave was the first doctor, the first scientist, that I had ever heard use the word 'magic' with respect. But then, Dr. Dave was the only doctor I'd known who was also a healer who swam with dolphins.

It was in the afternoon, when the sun was high over-head and tropically strong, that I would learn something else about teaching — something that transcended the ideal of teaching. Dr. Dave was once again holding Kevin in his arms while chest deep in the water. During this afternoon session, though, Kevin was not the same boy he was when he left DRC that morning. He was once again withdrawn and balled up in his wheelchair when he returned with his parents and his younger brother for his second session with Tursi.

When Dr. Dave asked Tursi for help, she did what she usually did to get Kevin's attention, but Kevin would not look up at her, no matter what feat she performed. "Kevin, pay attention!" Dr. Dave called. "Kevin, pay attention!" But Kevin would have nothing of it. He remained withdrawn in the doctor's arms. Maybe Kevin was thinking that the fun was over and that he was still stuck in that position, that no matter what the dolphins did, he would never change. Maybe fifteen-year-old Kevin had already encountered too many civilized-thinking, academic doctors who remained outside any spiritual experience and dimension. Maybe Kevin could still hear them telling his parents how he would never change, except for the worse. I have heard doctors crush even the smallest hope that can rise from despair, that tiny hope that humans need to keep going, even when that day's journey may lead into that long dark night.

Tursi withdrew.

"Kevin, pay attention," Dr. Dave pleaded. But with what was about to happen, Dr. Dave would be of little consequence. Tursi rose out of the water, eye level with Kevin. There was a slight pause; then she scooped up a mouthful of water, and sprayed it right into Kevin's face. Kevin snapped his head back and his face contorted. He seemed angry. Then, to his parents' surprise, Kevin smiled and raised his eyes to Tursi. She had his attention.

Simone, Carises, and I remained at DRC for two more days. For Simone, I had hoped that the good energy of the dolphins would help revitalize her own, and stimulate the desire to delve deeper into her past, back to a childhood that needed understanding and healing, a childhood shrouded by vague cancerous memories of drunken men, memories fueled by toxins and poisons that may have caused her young cells to mutate and her body-mind to program a kind of self-destruction, perhaps the same kind that beached cetaceans exhibit.

I had hoped that by watching and being around the

dolphins at DRC, Simone would experience the beauty of the innocence that she was denied and a rebirth of trust that could only come from somewhere deep inside her.

I had hoped that her stay at DRC would reaffirm the primal power of the indigenous female within her and that of Native American women in particular. By observing and learning what other life forms and beings, like the dolphins, had to teach, she would truly know that female power. For she discovered that dolphin societies are matrilineal, like her own people's, and most all other natural societies before the intrusion of male-dominated churches and civilized governments. She knew that it wasn't supposed to be her responsibility alone to protect her brothers and sisters from the same demented male source that robbed her of self-esteem and innocence. She learned that the welfare of dolphin young is shared by mothers and fathers and aunts and uncles and grandparents — just like Indians. Original Instruction teaches that all should take part and share in the raising of the future. And the future for these new primal souls should not be left to themselves, like it had been for her.

By watching Tursi and Talon, Simone also realized that she really was a good mother, that she had done right by her own children by keeping them home and assuming the role as their primary teacher. She hadn't thrown them into a civilized, male-dominated world to let strangers without direction themselves direct the lives of her children. She wanted her young to remain in her sphere of influence, one that would allow them a sense of purpose and identity, one that would allow them to experience the Original Instruction for themselves. Simone was like a dolphin mother.

When we returned to our St. Petersburg home, we shared our dolphin experiences with other people, especially with Sara, a sister in the spirit way and a Mohawk grandmother in the Old Way. I told Sara how the dolphins reconnected people to what is truly important in life — love for one's family, an appreciation for the blessings and even the struggles of our existence, and an acknowledgment that we share this world with other forms of living, feeling creatures.

I told her about Kevin, and she responded by telling me that what Tursi, the dolphin, had done with Kevin, the Mohawks used to do with their children. "When we couldn't get their attention, we'd spritz water in their faces. It worked. My mother did it to me. We don't have to scold our children, or strike them. We still do this to our dogs, in order to teach them how to behave. We spray water in their faces." Then she paused. "You know," she said, "I think we may have learned this from the dolphins a long, long time ago."

At one gathering in Tampa we shared conversation and stories with Indians from all over the Western Hemisphere. It was during this time that we heard the magical and mysterious dolphin stories of South

America, and we listened as the old women from the Amazon told us how the pink river dolphin still becomes a human and how he's sometimes sent to choose a human mate. They described to us in Spanish how he emerged from the water and walks ashore, wearing a hat or other type of head covering to conceal his blow hole. They described him standing under the waxing full moon while the drums pounded and the people danced. They described how he watched the flames of the central fire flicker upon the faces of the eligible pretty girls of the village, and how he lured the prettiest toward him. How that young woman gave birth to their child on the great river's shore, once again establishing the bond between the two species. "We know such a woman," they said.

Carises also established a bond with the dolphins — one that will last his lifetime. He returned home from DRC and drew dolphins, and his drawings brought him recognition and awards at a regional Native American art and education exhibition, as well as from our friends who would stop by and visit and be drawn to his pictures displayed on the walls of our living room. But, more than that, I believe his graceful line drawings of dolphins have also served to ignite the code of Original Instruction in many of those who saw his art. Perhaps that too was part of the plan and the purpose of our making this journey to the Florida Keys and DRC.

We watched the dolphins and became better aware of the beauty there is in living and the joy there is to life, even as our greatest challenge faced us, helping Simone deal with breast cancer. We would be reminded of what's most important in life: to live in harmony with each other and the environment we live in, to be thankful for the blessings of life and the time we have together, and to reflect this gratitude in our actions. We would learn to let go of the pettiness of this civilized world and to luxuriate in life's miracles. We would be reminded that this way of living is recorded somewhere deep inside us, at the core of our Original Instruction, and that the responsibilities of living in this Great Holy Mystery must be shared if we are to continue. We would become better aware of our connection to the web of life that Spider Woman had long ago created — and aware that in this web there are no superior beings, only equal parts that make up the whole.

Yesterday I saw a picture in a local newspaper of a tuna boat. The flag snapping in the wind above the mast could have been one from any number of civilized nations. Hanging upside down over the bow of the boat, suspended from two poles, were several dolphins. They were bottle-nose, the same species as those living at DRC. They were all dead. It was another moment of

Spiritus Mundi, when the collective unconscious gathers in one spot and generates its own kind of power. Two men stood alongside them in a pool of crimson. One held a long knife in his hand. The other leaned against one of the poles, posing. It was similar to the scene on the front page of that *Akwesasne Notes* newspaper over twenty years ago.

When I looked at that family of dead dolphins, something surfaced from my subconscious, and a Mayan poem came to mind. The poem prophesies the end of the world as the Mayans know it.

On that day, the tender leaf is destroyed,
On that day, the dying eyes are closed,
On that day, three signs are in the tree,
On that day, three generations hang there,
On that day, the battle flag is raised....

The words of this poem come from the forest of Chiapas, whose native people and trees are falling now before the artificial extensions of guns and machines, and the mentality of civilized men. It affirms what we taught at the AIM Survival School about how important it is for the old proven ways of seeing the world to live on. And we must never surrender those ways. Never!

CHAPTER 3

Paints Her Dreams

*Do not be afraid.... I am from a long time past, yet I
live today. I have traveled from the seven dancing stars
to teach you what many of Earth's people have forgotten. Listen, and you will remember!*

— Star Spirit, in
Ceremony in the Circle of Life

It was during Peace Time that I first saw the image of
Paints Her Dreams. Though the timing seems under-
standable to me now, it wasn't until later on, when I had
learned from her that War did not exist back then, that
it all began to make sense to me. War was only a monster in a dream — a dream she had as a young girl, back
when there were no people called Indians living here,
only the Calusa, and there was no land called Florida,
but only The Land Where the Wind Is Born....

She was a hazy form shimmering in the sunlight of a
warm December morning. She sat on bended knee

watching my children as they played along the water's edge. The beach was deserted except for clusters of quiet gulls gathered among the dunes, and an occasional line of brown pelicans that would swoop down just beyond the sandbar where small waves broke with an incoming tide. I wondered if I hadn't fallen asleep to the sounds of the waves and the playful laughter of the children and if upon my sudden awakening, my eyes were not adjusting well to the slant of a solstitial sun and its reflection off the gleaming green water of the Gulf....

She was barely visible in the soft sunlight of that warm winter morning, yet I could see that she was young and beautiful simply by the way she sat so gracefully upon her knees and watched so lovingly as the children played around her.

I wondered: Is this real? And then I was aware that I was sitting fully conscious in the bone-white sand, staring at her waist-length hair. I thought that maybe she was an Indian who had once lived in this place.

I questioned the meaning of her presence. Why did she want to be near my children? Then I wondered if perhaps she had once had children of her own, and if the sounds of playful laughter and the joy of native children had somehow brought her back from another world, another time, in the way that those same sounds and feelings lured me from my sleep. "The ghosts are of the land they love," Uncle Nip would say. Still I wondered if she had appeared for reasons I would never know.

I don't recall how long she remained there on the beach watching my children play, or exactly when she faded away. I know only that the hazy form that shimmered before my eyes that warm winter day was real enough to make me feel as though I wanted to know who she was. Maybe she was some connection to our past, or perhaps even to our future. I remember Uncle Nip telling me about past and future ghosts — how a ghost will manifest for good or bad reasons, how it is powerless to act, how it can only observe and evoke feelings among the living, feelings that can cause things to happen....

These were some of the thoughts that swirled through my mind then, even as Peace Day that year arrived.

My wife and I, along with our three children, who were all named for extinct peoples — Ihasha, six; Calusa, four; and Carises, two — were gathered in a circle near the Peace Tree, with our elder uncles, Nippawanock and his brother Metacomet, and some close family friends on the red brick-tiled living room floor of our home, playing "giveaway." The gust of an unusually warm tropical breeze would occasionally pass through the open jalousies of the front door.

"Your tree is lovely again this year," Nip commented to Simone and me, as he reached up to the tree behind him. He held one of the eagle feathers that hung from one of its synthetic branches in a strand of colorful beads.

"I strung the beads, Uncle," Calusa said. "Mommy helped me some."

"And a pretty strand it is, indeed, Calusa." Nip's

fingers ran the length of the beads. "You have a way of stringing pretty colors together — just like your mother. Each one blends into the next."

Then he turned to face the circle we had formed on the floor. In the middle was a pile of presents, all painstakingly wrapped but without cards to identify their owners. That was the idea, and why it was called the "giveaway." Uncle instructed each of us to take a turn and pick out a present from the pile. The one who picked the present would open it and then decide who in the circle should have it or would like to have it most. If the one who picked the present wanted it and gave it away, then the person it was given to could give it back. It was a game to help keep us aware of the things that could make one another happy and to help teach us generosity and to guard us against selfishness. It was also a lot of fun.

Such a tradition was always practiced among the People. "It's what made our nation strong," Uncle would say. "It's the kind of tradition that gave them identity."

This particular giveaway, though, was one that only occurred during the time of the winter solstice. That was what made it so special, for it allowed our children something to fill the void that Christmas and Hanukkah created for them. It brought back a native tradition that the missionaries had nearly stolen from the People's memory, a giving tradition to honor a special spirit that otherwise could have been forgotten. If a spirit no longer exists in the minds and hearts of the People, it can lose its power; it can even die. Uncle would explain that to keep this from happening we should honor the spirit of Nokomo this time of year. He said that we should invite Nokomo into our home, for Nokomo is the Spirit of Giving.

Peace Time was also an occasion that reminded us of our connection to cosmic events and to family ties of love and sharing, not only among people, but among our other relatives, all of the earth's other life forms. This time of peace also helped us recall our connection to Mother Earth. "It is a rare time, however brief," Nip would say, "when the world is at peace."

Nip also showed us how to use the winter solstice to teach the children their native history, and to tell them the stories of how our people found ways to live in peace, so that peace, not war, became a way of life.

And so we would start telling the children, before they even understood the meanings of the words, the stories about the native Peacemakers who walked the Americas before the white man came. We would tell them about the virgin birth of Deganawida, "a true prince of peace," and about his work with the great orator Hyonwatha in establishing the Law of Great Peace among the Iroquois. We would tell them how the Iroquois uprooted a great pine and, into the cavity it left, into the depths of the undercurrents far below the earth, cast all weapons of war forever. We would tell them how the great pine was replanted among the People of the Longhouse and from then on was called the Tree of Peace.

We would tell them the story about the White

Buffalo Woman and how she brought the Buffalo Calf
Pipe to the Sioux. How she instructed men and women
to form a circle of love and peace when they smoked
from the sacred pipe.

We would tell them stories about the People who
lived across the waters of the Gulf. How, long ago,
Quetzalcoatl descended from the sky as a feathered serpent. How he took the form of a man who discouraged
human sacrifice and revitalized the People's arts. We
explained to the children, in the way that Uncle Nip had
explained to us, how Quetzalcoatl had shown the ancestors of the Aztecs and Mayans that, through creativity,
their people could demonstrate their gratitude to the
Giver of Life in ways other than human sacrifice. Uncle
Nip said that the Feathered Serpent's influence was so
strong that Aztec and Mayan art and knowledge
became something the world had never before seen or
known. He said that the art that they created out of love
and gratitude has never been surpassed.

"It's about peace and giving," Simone and I would
tell the children, and I would feel those ties to the primal
past grow stronger inside me — grow stronger inside us.

As the children grew to understand the meanings of
these words, we would also teach them about the sacred
symbolism of the decorations that hung from the artificial pine we called the Peace Tree. It was artificial, we
explained, because we did not believe in killing a tree for
a decoration, no matter how meaningful we might
attempt to make it. We told our children that we didn't
want a tree dying a slow death in our home. "After all,"

Simone would say, "look at all that the Tree nations have given to us. How could we kill one of our tree relatives for a decoration this week, then discard it like trash the next?"

Ihasha was a year old when Uncle Nip first stood by the Peace Tree, holding him in one arm while pointing with his free hand to each item hanging from the tree's branches of metal and soft nylon needles. "The feathers are for the winged nations of the earth," Nip said. "And the colorful balls are for the round things of the universe: the earth, the sun, the moon, the planets." Nip lifted a strand of popcorn and touched it to Ihasha's hand. "These strings of popped corn," he said, "represent the foods of the earth." Then he held up the deer hooves. "These," he said, "represent the animals that have served our people unselfishly as teachers and providers." Then he looked up toward the top of the tree. The eyes of the child in his arms followed his. "And the silver star you see up there is placed above us to remind us of our ancestors and our special relationship to the stars."

The giveaway game just added to the fun and to the learning and to everything else on Peace Day. When it had ended and the wrappings were all gathered up, I glanced over at Uncle Nip. He had retired to the soft rattan chair near the Peace Tree. He was perspiring. His face seemed flushed. "Are you okay, Uncle?" I asked.

He nodded and smiled. "Fine" he said. "I'm just fine."

I turned my gaze around the room at my wife and

our friends and our children — all engaged in quiet conversation or play. It was at that moment, when I once again felt the warm gust of an unusual winter's day — this time sweeping through the front door and around us all — that I remembered her, and I suddenly had an overwhelming sense of love and family. Such a moment made everything seem more special to me. "Why is this so, Uncle Nip? Why does it feel so special this time?" I asked.

"Because you're becoming aware that these times are not going to last forever, nephew. There won't be many more."

I reached into my pocket and pulled out a shard of old pottery. I rubbed it with my thumb as I clutched it in my palm. Then I handed it to Nip.

"What do you think?" I asked. "It was given to me the other day by one of the park rangers. He said it was like no other piece found in the area. He told me its design and black color were so unusual that no one could figure out what tribe it came from." Nip held it up and studied it. "The ranger said I could keep it for as long as I needed, to see if I could learn anything about it, maybe even in a psychic kind of way. Is that crazy, Uncle? I mean, I'm no psychic."

Nip held it some more and examined it for a long time. He rubbed it again and again.

"Did anything unusual happen...recently?" he asked. Another warm breeze swept through the front door. It lifted some of the decorative balls hanging from the tree, and rushed past me.

"I saw something on the beach the other day. I think maybe it was a ghost."

Nip handed the old pottery piece to me. "Was it in the morning...around nine?"

I told him that it was, but I concealed my surprise when he mentioned the correct time. I told him that I was certain the ghost was that of a young maiden. He nodded slightly. His lips tightened, and he seemed for a moment to be looking within himself. "I know who it was," he said. "And someday I'll tell you. But not now. Now isn't the time."

I asked why he couldn't reveal her identity to me now. He just shook his head and said that if he died before that could happen, Uncle Met would tell me.

The rest of that winter was a difficult one; I felt uncomfortable and morose. I slept restlessly. The winter weather turned bitter by Florida standards, too. It took its toll on the weak and the old. A freeze nearly wiped out the orange groves. Cold air toward spring almost ruined the March strawberry harvest. And Uncle Nip had a heart attack. His surgery went well, but he said that he'd never go through it again.

Spring finally arrived. Cold waves from the north turned into warm ones from the Gulf. The children and I spent many of our days back on the beach, riding and playing among the white foamy crests of the Gulf's waves. That's when she returned....

She appeared standing between two small dunes, among the tall stalks of golden sea oats. Her form was barely discernible, but I recognized it just the same. Her long hair shimmered as she blurred and soon faded away.

When we came home that afternoon, the children headed outside to play, and I went into the bedroom, where I fell onto the bed, thinking about her. The slight hum of the ceiling fan and the soft rattle of sable fronds outside the open bedroom windows made the room feel warm and peaceful. It was very tranquil. . . .

I don't recall falling asleep. I don't recall lifting the mattress and getting out the pottery piece I had shared with Uncle Nip that winter. It's the voice I heard beckoning me that I remember. The voice and what I saw as I lifted free of my body and floated through. . . .

Time is of the Mystery. It's not something artificially measured by a clock. It doesn't flow in a straight line beginning at one point and ending at another. Time moves in circles and cycles in which events endlessly intertwine.

I found myself traveling like a spirit over her village. Below, I could see the thatched homes where her people lived. They were built on rows of mounds, clustered among sables and pines not far from the water's edge. I could see smoke rising from the fires that burned inside and outside the lodges. Myriad fish moved about in the clear emerald water. I could see the children playing. . . .

That's when I became more aware of her voice. All along this spirit-journey she had been speaking to me. The language was hers, yet I could feel its meaning, and somehow understand things with my heart that my head could not explain. I know now that what I was seeing was the way things were before she had her dream, before the monsters of War and Disease came for her.

I lay gazing up at the ceiling fan. I held the shard of pottery in my hand. Moonlight filtered through the sables outside the bedroom window, casting shadows on the wall that played with the spinning blades. How long had I been gone? How long would I feel the pain that comes when you lose someone close? How long would I feel lonely for a time that no longer exists?

Truth and the need to tell it could help manifest a ghost. There's no other way I can explain it. For five years I struggled to hear the ghost's voice and tell her story. For five years I had felt haunted by the memories she gave to me. I finally wrote her story the way it came to me, only Uncle Nip wrote the last line of the telling, the way it came to him.

"The children grow like Florida weeds," he said on the last Peace Day he would see them playing on the shore. The sun was the color of an orange as we watched it set over the Gulf. Simone sat on one side of him and I sat on the other. Uncle Met was too ill to be there.

You know the feeling that comes when you're totally aware of the moment you're living in? When you're aware that our time on the earth is so short? That clarity of feeling wrapped itself around me. I savored everything: the color of the sky, the thin layer of cirrus floating like white feathers across it, the emerald shade of the water, the laughter of the children. . . .

"There won't be many more like this, huh, Uncle?" I said, staring at the sun. I guess I needed the affirmation that I was, indeed, understanding something about life that I couldn't decipher so many Peace Times ago. Or maybe I was hoping he'd say, "No, just a few."

Nip watched the children on the shore as if he were etching into some soul-memory how they looked that lovely winter's day. "The water is always," he whispered softly to me.

"Yes, Uncle," I said. "The water is always."

Nippawanock died a week after that Peace Day in 1987. He never got to tell me who she was, nor did my Uncle Met, who died soon after. She called herself Paints Her Dreams in the story I wrote. And though Uncle Nip didn't reveal what he knew about her before he died, he did read the story. It was on Thanksgiving night, after he'd had a quarrel about Christianity with Princess Red Wing, his adopted mother. Red Wing was the direct descendant of Osamekun, the Massasoit who befriended the Pilgrims, and of his son Metacomet, called King Philip, who was forced to involve himself in the war that bears his name.

And though it was the unspoken rule that he and Red Wing did not argue over religion in Uncle's house, that night became an exception, perhaps because Nip understood that death was the shadow that had come to him that autumn, and there was too little time left to be tolerant of conflicting ideas and the people who would be so bold as to speak them in his presence. It could have been that he and Red Wing argued over Christianity because he recalled with clarity those early days on Quapaw land when he became "the son of that half-breed," and the only women who would take care of him while his mother worked were the local prostitutes in the Oklahoma mining town of Pitcher.

Perhaps he argued with Princess Red Wing that night because he was remembering the time the Christians took scissors to his hair and forbade him to speak "the language of the devil." Or maybe he had simply learned enough of their pious words and experienced enough of their inhuman behavior. Maybe it was one or none of these things that sparked and fueled the bitter argument that Thanksgiving night when he told Princess Red Wing that, after all the horror Christians had inflicted on our people, to support or believe in what they did was like dying. He said that their missionaries had taught us to think only of ourselves. He said they had taught us to reject our belief in the Great Holy Mystery. He said they had taught us that the earth was not our mother, that animals had no souls. He said that their religion had cleared the path for the monster of war. He said this after the television news had just reported the slaughter of an entire Indian village in Guatemala.

It was very late and stormy that night when Uncle Nip scribbled a notation on the back of the last page of the story, which was titled "A Piece of Pottery." He said that reading it had made him cry, for he had discovered that Princess Red Wing and Paints Her Dreams had something in common. Even though he never told me outright what he knew about Paints Her Dreams, he did write the final line of her story. It haunts me still....

"He cried for a beautiful maiden sacrificed."

Author's Note:

"A Piece of Pottery," the story within "Paints Her Dreams," was sent to Sylvia Tankel of *Short Story International*, where it was published that same year, the year Uncle Nip died — 1987. I never saw Paints Her Dreams again.

CHAPTER 4

Ancestors Among the Stars

There will soon come a time when a light man or light men will appear on the earth. They will have the capability to stop atomic power and electricity. I shiver to think about it. But too much electricity and atomic power are being used and they make the world out of balance.... This light man or men will also have the power to do good. This will happen before this century is over.

— Lame Deer
Lame Deer: Seeker of Visions

When ships of light move across the ocean of space, cutting at seemingly impossible angles, zooming at unimaginable speeds...when they travel into our sleep and take us beyond the moon, far past the sun, and into the outer reaches of the sea of galaxies...when they transcend into mystical entities before us, and we are not dreaming but fully conscious and aware, then it is time to acknowledge our relationship to the stars.

Carises came to me early one morning and found me outside, standing on the front patio, watching the sunrise, contemplating the stars. It had been a disturbing night for my youngest son. It had also been one for me, also, and for Simone.

Though only a few hours had passed since it happened, I still felt the shock from waking up in our bed with someone or something standing over me. It was the dead of night and I had been in what I thought was a deep sleep. I awoke in sudden terror. It was as if some force was pressing on me, making me lie back down. I called out my wife's name, but she would not awaken. In an instant, I sprang to the edge of the bed and sat, "strumming the lute" — muscles tense, motioning instinctively with my arms and hands, the quivering sound of my breath, the energy of T'ai Chi flowing.

A long, spindly looking spirit-being floated before me, and imitated the sequence. In this kind of body language, the entity had assured me that he would not hurt me, for while such a maneuver enables one the ultimate striking potential, it can be utilized only in self-defense.

What was I seeing?
Even before my eyes fully opened and I could form the question, even before I jolted to the edge of the bed, the answer had already formed in my subconscious. For there is that exact moment when truth is like an ember separating from its source, a spark emerging from the

farthest star. It is an instant, a flash in the deep primordial recesses of the mind, a flicker of light where pure thought crystallizes in those vast unexplored regions of inner space. And it can be terrifying, for it is an awareness that illuminates some long-ago memory of the distant past, casting ominous shadows on the puzzling present.

And it was in that awful and wonderful moment that I called out the name of my wife. She had been sleeping alongside me that night as she had nearly every night for the past fifteen years. "Simone! Simone!" I cried, but she wouldn't answer. "Do you see him? Do you see him?" But she didn't move. She didn't turn to see the entity, and though I did not consciously understand why, I somehow knew that she couldn't. She remained silent and still.

"Alas," she would write in her journal later on, regarding the experience, "I saw only blackness and was unable to gather the wherewithal to respond in any way, except to look as the voices in the darkness had commanded. But in my sleep?

"I recall how unusual I thought the sounds of those voices were as they talked on my left and slightly behind me. I recall seeing three circles of black before me."

She described stepping through the first one and going toward the second when she heard me cry her name. "I could hear you," she said, "but I couldn't respond."

Then she told how the voices talked to her about her interior self, her "inner space"...the power of her dreams... and how she could recover psychic powers if she wished. The implication was that she would recover something she used to have. "Desire and consciousness seemed to be important," she said. "I was there but did not see what you wanted me to see — I saw only blackness — the circles.... And I can remember a strange sensation on my skin as I stepped through the first circle and toward the second." In her journal she would describe it "like a liquid, but a shiver. Strange. So strange."

She returned from dream-time and the black rings, startled by an exploding light just outside the window near our bed. She raised her head from the pillow and turned in time to see me rushing out the door. She grabbed a sheet and followed me outside reluctantly, for she knew what I'd see. It was something we had discussed many times in order to come to terms with its presence. We agreed that it does not have a name, for a name would diminish its potential. It is mysterious. It is unknown. And as we surrendered to our fears, we turned in the direction of its light....

She found me naked in the dark standing alongside a palm tree, staring up at an unusual and low circular cloud in an otherwise cloudless sky. It glowed in an eerie kind of way and remained stationary just above our house for as long as it seemed we needed to experience it. Then it dissipated and disappeared as if the whole incident had been some unusual kind of dream that Simone and I had shared and had simultaneously awakened from, a dream that had somehow crossed the fine line of the unconscious.

That morning on the patio I suggested to my son Carises that maybe we really had dreamed our experiences, but Carises wouldn't agree. He stood alongside me, motioning with his small hands to demonstrate their light buoyant movement, telling me how ghost-like people had come into his bedroom and floated him away. "It was as if they came through the window, Dad."

The experiences of that night were repeated at different times and in different ways for the remainder of the summer. Once, on a clear July day, Simone, the children and I were playing together in the Gulf, luxuriating in the moment of family when, from the direction of the land, something shot toward us — traveling at such a speed that we couldn't make out its form. We only glimpsed something moving at phenomenal speed, and heard the powerful "whoosh" that followed it.

And later that same month, we stood on the shore watching a cigar-shaped, silvery white object drift slowly along the horizon. Then it paused and sort of collapsed in on itself, became a black dot, and disappeared.

My daughter Calusa also had an experience. It happened on an August morning when she was out trying to rescue a bird for the Wild Bird Rescue and Rehab

Center located down the street. She said she saw a triangular-shaped object shoot over the bay and out into the Gulf. She was so excited about it that Simone asked her to draw a picture of what she saw.

As a result of all the incidents that summer, Simone and I began remembering others that had occurred just before and shortly after the children were born. But our memories seemed fragmented and barely discernible, like we were looking through a thick haze. A lot of the details of our experiences were just not there. Still, we were amazed that it had taken so many years for any aspect of something so extraordinary to rise to our consciousness. This troubled Simone. I know it did. For the remembered experiences took place during her pregnancies.

It also frightened her to know that somehow our children were involved after they were born. For Simone was, above all else, a mother, and because these visitations didn't require her conscious permission, they violated her instinctive nature to protect her children. Regardless of any good that "the Star People" could bring to our Mother Earth, the very idea of them in our lives was unnerving. Years later, I would read from one of her journal entries the impact that they had on her life. "Maybe they are the best friends I could ever have," she wrote. "Friends with the courage to be hard on me in order to help me grow. . . . But they are so terrifying."

She would add how they came across as "very negative" to her. But then she would describe how the whole universe exists because of friction between negative and positive. How atomic friction causes the heat and light of the stars. How positive and negative forces battle perpetually. "This is a simple physical reality," she stated. "Does that make negative forces evil? No, it makes them essential."

I appreciated Simone's insights about them, and understood her anxiety as well. Though I regarded the incidents around them with more enthusiasm, I too was afraid. Yet as frightened as I was the night I encountered that strange entity suspended in the air before me, I somehow welcomed and accepted the idea that he or they were, indeed, here. And I think that this acceptance was true for all of us to some degree. For each of us was feeling a special kind of awareness of our connection to the stars. And though a few of the incidents were frightening, we each accepted the unspoken — that we were, in fact, having experiences that went beyond our present abilities to comprehend.

Perhaps all this was part of some kind of selective group phenomena where familiar thought forms are shared and in this way become manifest. Or perhaps the light or ghost-like entities that we experienced really do exist outside our human thoughts. Maybe they do come from another world, maybe even another universe, or maybe they come from another dimension and can pass through to this one because they know where to find the doors.

The possibilities are endless, and they can stretch our imaginations beyond the limits we set. Still, as Native Americans we had no choice but to accept the notion that these "Star People" were, in fact, reality and that they had somehow become an integral part of our family life. What helped us the most was our concept of the Great Holy Mystery, for we were taught by our uncle and other elders of the People that we are part of an incomprehensible universe, and in a universe beyond our human comprehension, anything is possible — anything.

As I look on it now, it was the condition of our planet that perhaps had made it so easy for us to deal with their intrusion into our lives. After all, it was apparent after each war, especially after the Gulf War that our children watched on television, that humans were capable of doing the most heinous and horrific things to the earth, to each other, and to other life forms. Television images of the burning black smoke of the oil fields of Kuwait, of the bodies of the dead Iraqi soldiers rotting alongside desert roads, and of the overwhelming numbers of the innocent birds and fish covered in black, tarry goo washed up on the shore of ebony, oil-stained beaches affirmed the need of some kind of supernatural intervention to stop the madness.

I have often wondered if perhaps these Star People are here to alter human behavior by somehow manipulating or stimulating our genetic code, or maybe altering the genetic code of specific people. Maybe Simone was on to something when she questioned in her journal why they come across so negatively; perhaps that's what this is all about. Perhaps they are catalysts in our evolutionary journey. Maybe they are the ones the ancient indigenous Peruvians honored on the Plains of Nasca where they etched into the earth the image of the tail of a great monkey that separates into an ascending spiral that can only be seen from the sky. Or maybe they are the ones represented by the Katchinas of the Hopi, or the Shalakos of the Zuni in the Southwest. Maybe these Star People are the ones depicted by the ancient Anasazi on the rock walls of places like Pueblo Bonito.

Native Americans know that this wouldn't be the first time supernatural beings appeared on earth and aided humans. Names like Quetzalcoatl, Deganawida, Manco Capac, and White Buffalo Calf Woman intertwine with the collective history and unique cultures of America's native people. These sacred beings influenced great leaps in spiritual and social growth, with elements of mystery and magic in their virgin or otherwise unusual origins, and in their departures. The old stories that describe Quetzalcoatl descending from the sky as a plumed serpent, or the Seneca Creation Account that tells of a woman who fell from the sky, these and other stories are now regarded as myths among civilized people, but they are not unlike what we experience today with the Star People and UFO sightings seen all over the world. Perhaps old myths are coming to life again, or perhaps new ones are being born.

So, if our family could provide any assistance in our development as a people and as a species, and benefit our great Mother Earth, then we would try to ease our fears of these strange beings who came into our sleeping and waking lives. I wonder if maybe that's what Uncle

Nip meant the day we spoke of UFOs, and he said to let it be. As frightening and as intrusive as they are, maybe we must simply learn to accept their existence and their impact in our lives. For maybe they really are part of our spiritual and social growth, and by assisting in our evolution, they really can help the earth. This possibility warrants respect and is something to contemplate, and even celebrate.

Simone described their existence simply and elegantly: "They truly are Manitou," she said, meaning simply, they truly are . . . of the Mystery.

And though each of us feels that we'll never fully comprehend what or who the Star People are in such a civilized world or what their relationship is to primal people, we grow content with the spiritual acceptance that comes from that ancient belief: what the children of the earth do not comprehend as they walk the paths of life will become clear to them only when they pass into the mysteries of Wah-kon-tah.

But the civilized mind cannot understand such spiritual acceptance, so the civilized world tries to explain the idea of the Star People away or, worse yet, because of its greed, the idea of Star People is demeaned into something marketable. And though our experiences as a family remained within a close circle of our own people and special friends, the civilized world began toying with "alien encounters" and UFOs like never before. Hollywood joined in, producing films with friendly caricatures in *Close Encounters of the Third Kind* and *ET*, or more terrifying ones, like *Alien* and *Fire in the Sky*, the latter a sinister fictionalized rendition of a true story. Such ideas only emphasize the conflict between primal and civilized thought.

Following the months of that incredible summer, we would see UFOs shoot across our television set via videotaped encounters over Florida and other places throughout the world. We would learn how some astronauts experienced them. And on one local Tampa Bay broadcast on WTVT, Channel 13, UFOs were recorded live. I remember watching the digital seconds of the video camera's clock flicking away in the corner of our TV screen as an entity of light moved about in the night sky above the shoreline of Gulf Breeze in the midst of excited human voices.

During and after that particular summer, it seemed as though there was at least an incident a week reported and/or investigated on one tabloid news program or another. A local television station ran several shows dealing with UFOs.

Alien encounters, crop circles, and UFO incidents became so thoroughly discussed by such a diversity of people that even conservative mainstream TV picked up on the phenomena, and felt the idea of UFOs worthy of a *48 Hours* program. And, by then, Whitley Streiber's book *Communion* had become a major bestseller.

It seemed that nearly every time we turned on the

television Simone and I and the children would catch film clips from the space shuttle, home videos, and media sightings of crafts of light moving about the skies of the earth. We watched televised interviews conducted by a Harvard professor with people who said they had been abducted by extraterrestrials. We saw eerie photographs of bizarre cattle mutilations. We would listen to the theories about how aliens were abducting innocent people and experimenting on them in the most malevolent ways. Of course what they were claiming was exactly how human scientists treat animals. We would hear the projected fear in the alleged victims' voices and see the real or pretended terror in their eyes, or we would observe the ridicule and demeaning natures of those more civilized humans who couldn't allow the idea of any kind of life form to exist outside of their own limited perceptions.

But what does a father like me say to his youngest son on the patio while we share a sunrise and discuss unusual events that happened during the night? Carises was becoming frightened and wanted to know more than what the civilized mass media was presenting. He needed some kind of understanding, something he could grasp hold of, something that could help him make sense out of all this. What can a father say to his child about such things, especially when curiosity quivers in a soft voice and my own comprehension is so limited?

What did an elder uncle once say to his young nephew when the young nephew asked about UFOs? I can recall the moment clearly. It was after the time I'd seen a wheel of colorful light in another kind of starry sky, one that was over an ancient Timacuan sun temple mound near our home in Safety Harbor. Our eldest son, Ihasha, was still a baby, and Simone was pregnant with Calusa. After I saw the wheel that night, I began writing my first children's story, *Ceremony in the Circle of Life*. While visiting with Uncle Nip in Tampa shortly after that experience with the wheel, I felt the need to ask him what he thought about such things as UFOs.

It was Thanksgiving Day. We had just finished doing the dishes together. I remember how he paused in the kitchen doorway, how he stood for a moment, as if contemplating a careful response. Not wanting to put him in an uncomfortable situation, I turned to leave. I figured that maybe this was something he really didn't want to discuss, yet I knew that he was an avid science fiction reader. He even taught sci-fi and fantasy at the university. That's when he touched my arm. I looked back and he looked at me. His lips were tight and his eyes were penetrating but not intrusive. "Let it be," he said firmly. Then he said it again almost sympathetically. "Let it be." And that's all he ever said on the subject, and he walked away.

But later that same year he would help me to understand why I chose the Pleiades to write about in *Ceremony in the Circle of Life*, and why I described these spirits coming to earth to teach the earth's children what they had forgotten. Uncle Nip told me that the Cherokee, like many other Native people, have stories about the Pleiades. He said they were part of the oral literature of the People, but that some of them were recorded now in the literature of the written word as well.

Perhaps if Uncle Nip had lived a little longer we would have had interesting discussions about UFOs and crop circles and what they mean regarding our relationship to the stars, to the earth, and to our ancestors. Or perhaps Uncle Nip was concerned that I not become obsessed with having to know what they really are and what they're doing in our lives. Such obsession could obscure truth. It could keep me from walking and living the path of my heart. It could distort my judgment regarding whatever I might discover. I could even bring ridicule or harsh skepticism, or worse, upon myself and my family, which even as I write these words has an ominous ring. "Let it be," he said. Yet he would still nudge me toward the books that contained the stories.

And though I must acknowledge that those three words served a purpose then, I felt it difficult to say them to Carises that morning on the patio. After all, how could I let it be when he was so afraid? How could I give to my youngest son, and each of my children, something more than civilized theories and Hollywood images? In one way I could tell him to "Let it be" for the same reasons Uncle Nip had told me. But in another way I wanted to give my children a sense of peace about these experiences. Though I contemplated the right thing to do, one thing was certain: I couldn't tell Carises that what happened the night before was only a dream, because he comes from a primal culture that was guided and inspired by dreams. And I couldn't tell my youngest son that there was no magic in the world, or that the universe was something humans really did understand.

I knew that I would not find the answers in memories of conversations about UFOs or Star People with Uncle Nip, so I did what my uncle had shown me with his wordless actions, and I turned to our bookshelves that housed the books where the stories dwelled. Somewhere among those pages of culture and history, I knew the stories existed; stories about beings who traveled from the stars and the humans they encountered. Ancient stories. Tribal stories recorded over time. Stories told long ago in the oral tradition. Stories about Creation. Stories about time travel. And stories about love.

That night, I found one of those stories. Before the children went to sleep, I lit a candle in their bedroom and shut off the lights. I suggested that they imagine that the candle was a fire and their bedroom was a wigwam.

Shadows danced and gestured on the walls around us as I opened the book. I scooted alongside my youngest son's bed, and found the page where the story began. The children were sleepy, especially Carises, for the dreamy visitations and the eerie experiences of the past summer almost always came in the dead of night, so the children had been staying up later and later. Carises even pulled several all-nighters. So, as the flickering firelight made dark dancing shapes on the wigwam walls, I began to read the story of Eshkebug and Sky Woman, and as I read, the magic of a mystery began to unfold. . . .

This is my retelling of the story, based on several different renditions I have heard and read.

Eshkebug and the Star Maiden

It began in a tiny and remote village along the shore of the Great Water that the Anishinabe (the Original People) called Gitchie Gumme. A handsome young man lived in a wigwam alone with his mother and his father. And though he was approaching manhood, he would not be considered as such until he had earned an adult name. That would come only as a result of a vision quest. Should he get much older and not seek the vision, the People would regard him as a man who wandered through life without direction and purpose. He would simply be known as a man without a vision. Without such a quest, the handsome young man would be something akin to a half-man, and one the People could never fully trust.

So, as the young man approached his sixteenth cycle of seasons, he went to his parents and told them that he was ready. Seeking a vision in the Old Way was something they had prepared him for most of his young life. Yet, for all the physical training needed to develop the strength and endurance necessary for such a quest, it was the heart of the individual that signaled the intent and the time.

It was a spring long ago in the days of the First People, and the blessings of life were everywhere. They seemed more evident than ever to the young man as he wandered deep through the forest alone without eating or drinking. He wandered among the birches and pines for a full day until he reached the tree line that opened to a grassy slope. He climbed the knoll slowly to the top and then stood silent, savoring the beauty that had unfolded before him. A field of wild flowers exploded in colors where the hills around him formed a little valley. It was near this field, among the flowers, that the young man fasted and prayed, day after day.

The sky on the final night of his quest was filled with stars, more than he had ever imagined. In his mind's eye, he followed a misty star trail that stretched from horizon to horizon across the universe, a trail his people called the Path of Souls.

Three days passed in his quest, and he wondered more and more about his vision. Were his mind wanderings among the stars part of it? He recognized that he did become more aware of his connection to the sky, to the earth, and to the beauty he shared with other forms of life. He wondered if this awareness was part of his vision, for he had heard that some visions were subtle and didn't occur at once. He had heard a story of one vision that came in parts over the course of the person's entire life. He had also been taught that a vision may take a lifetime to live and to understand, and even then one may never fully comprehend its significance.

The handsome young Ojibway had sensed his own humility when he traveled among the Standing Nations — those trees that had lived for hundreds, even thousands, of years on this earth. And he had luxuriated in the lovely scent permeating the rainbow field of flowers, and smiled at the myriad of colorful and ephemeral butterflies that paused there, like him, to take it all in. Is this my vision? he wondered.

And though he journeyed on this quest alone, his heart knew no loneliness, for he felt more connected to the world, more aware of that part of himself that connected him to all things, than ever in his life. He sensed the center of the universe inside him, and he understood that the same center was in everything he saw.

During the last night of his vision quest, he watched the stars moving across the heavens. He imagined them as living entities of spirit-light moving through the ocean of space, swept across the void by stellar winds. He recognized and focused on the cluster of seven stars within the great trail, and remembered the old stories about the Star People who moved across the night sky.

But stars don't move about like that, the young man whispered, as if the conscious part of his mind was in conflict with the unconscious.

No sooner had the conscious thought been formed into words that he realized how little he knew about such things. How little he knew about the world. Yet he wanted to know.... If he was to have a purpose among his People and a direction on this earth, he wanted to know all he could about his world. He wanted to know about the universe. He wanted to know more about himself. These were the thoughts he took into his sleep that last night of his vision quest, while entities of light moved sporadically above him, like sparks from a fire burning deep within in his spirit-mind.

When the young man awoke that dawn, he went to the stream that wound around the outer edges of the field of flowers. It was the fourth day, and he squatted by the stream, contemplating the taste of the water and how it would feel on his parched, dried lips. For the past few days he had reflected on his life — on all the good he had received. Now he felt so pitiful, because he didn't see how he could give anything back. He didn't see his purpose. In a weakened state, he wept.

That's when he observed the blurry image of a bright light green leaf, the color of early spring, floating on the surface of the stream before him. He watched transfixed as the leaf drifted across the image of a great stag, staring back at him from under the water. The antlers were like none the young man had ever seen. They were huge, like the twisting branches of wild oaks. And the eyes of the deer were deep, dark, and penetrating. They were of the Mystery, and the young man understood that he was, indeed, in the presence of something truly Manitou.

"You have always respected us," the deer said as the human form gazed down at him in the water. "Whenever we sacrificed our lives to your relatives for sustenance, you always thanked our spirit. Because you care for us and respect that which animates us and gives us life, and because you acknowledge us in this way, I bestow on you the power to become like us."

When the young man turned to see the deer reflected in the water, he saw nothing. When he glanced back at the flowing water of the stream, he saw only the bright green leaf riding away on the ripples.

He stood, bewildered, weak, and confused. He staggered among the flowers, heading toward a rim where he thought the magical deer might have gone, but when he reached the top, he saw nothing but the colorful flowers glistening with dew and pretty butterflies sparkling in the early morning light. Yet there was something unusual in the middle of the field. He gazed about and noticed that the flowers were pressed down. He traced the pattern of the impression with his eyes and walked among them. The flowers were not harmed in any way, just pressed closer to the earth, as if something had pushed down on them gently enough not to hurt them but firmly enough to form a circle. It was almost as if the flowers had become their own basket.

When he returned to his village, fatigued and hungry, his mother and his aunts prepared the feast that would break his fast. After he savored his first drink and delighted in the food, he sat near a warm fire while his father and uncles listened to the telling of the events of his quest. They uttered agreement and smiled as he recounted what the deer had told him. The elders who shared the fire with him that day helped him to better understand his newly gifted power of transformation. They also agreed that he had earned the right to receive a name that would identify him as a man, a name that would forever connect him to his vision. The elders told him that he was, indeed, a man of the People, a man who could be trusted. They would forever call him Eshkebug (New Leaf).

The following spring when Eshkebug was hunting, he saw a familiar light floating like a disconnected star across the azure sky. It reminded him of what he'd seen the last night of his vision quest, only this one seemed larger, closer. He watched until the floating light descended and disappeared in the direction of the field where he had once slept among the flowers, near the place where he had his first vision of the deer in the clear, flowing water.

As he approached the field where the light had settled, he could hear an unusual sound, like music, emanating from that direction. He followed the lure of the music until it stopped, just as he came to the edge of the woods. He saw a great light and moving shadows, and he quickly found cover behind a stand of birches. The light and shadows became form, and he saw several beautiful maidens walking among the flowers. Behind them was the craft of light that had brought them.

Eshkebug watched as the seven star maidens moved about, touching each flower as he'd seen the young mothers of his village often touch their newborns. Yet there was another force besides gentle affection at work here, for he also observed how warily they moved among the flowers, stroking their fingers on the stems and petals as if the flowers might contain some kind of hidden danger. He observed the midnight eyes of the maidens looking about carefully, suspicious of any danger that might lay concealed around them. He listened as the star maidens talked among the flowers, their voices whispers in the wind. And though he did not understand anything they said, he enjoyed the gentleness of their discourse. They reminded him of the times in the woods at night when he was a baby snuggled in a cradleboard on his mother's back, listening to the soft conversations of the People. How alert they were. How aware. How quiet.

Eshkebug continued to watch and listen until his attention focused on only one of the maidens. She strayed a little distance from the others, closer to where Eshkebug stood behind the birches. She closed her eyes and lifted her head to the warm, fragrant breeze. She smiled in its warmth. And it was at that moment that something indescribable happened to Eshkebug. His mind suddenly became aware of his heart in a way he had never known. At that moment Eshkebug knew that he would never set eyes on anything more beautiful than the lovely young maiden standing before him.

Wonderful feelings emerged, strange feelings that excited him, feelings that warmed him, feelings that made him aware of his manhood.

As the young star maiden continued to explore the flowers, she had unknowingly come even closer to Eshkebug. He could breathe her scent, as sweet as the flowers she walked among. It caused his heart to pound so strongly that he wondered if she might hear it. Then what? What if she saw him? Would she become frightened? Would she think of him only in a fearful way?

As quickly as these thoughts formed in his mind, they floated away until all but two remained: he wanted to know her; he wanted her to know him.

So, with one hand raised and opened and his other holding his bow at his side, Eshkebug stepped from behind the birch trees. His smile, his gentle gesture of peace, and something she saw in his eyes momentarily kept the beautiful maiden from running in terror, but when her gaze fell on the bow at Eshkebug's side and the quiver stocked with arrows strapped to his back, her instincts prevailed. In that instant Eshkebug's smile dropped, for he recognized his failure. He tried to utter an explanation, but she quickly fled to the other star maidens who swept her away. Before he could take a step in their direction, and plead his good intent, the star maidens were back in the craft already lifting from the ground and speeding into the bright sky.

When Eshkebug returned home, he described the incident to his mother. He told her about the craft of light and about the beautiful maidens who traveled in it. He told her that one of them had made his heart feel alive with new and unusual feelings. He told her that he longed for the company of this maiden and that he would not rest until he could be with her. He told her he wanted her for his.

Eshkebug's mother listened to her son's recounting of the event. While he described what he had seen and how he felt toward the star maiden, she remembered old stories, stories told among the People long ago.

When he finished, there was silence. Then she spoke.

"It is not good to love such a being, Eshkebug," she said. "I remember my grandmother telling me that. This maiden who stirs your feelings comes from another world. She is too frightened of humans to ever understand your good intentions. You can never come close enough to tell her how you feel. Even if you could speak with her, it would not be a good thing to have such a wife. Should this one you have fallen in love with ever grow to love you in return and even grow to like it here among our people, she would soon be lonely for her own kind. My grandmother said that Star People feel about the world they are from the way our people do about this world. This star maiden would long for her mother world. You could never bring true happiness to such a being."

The truthful words of Eshkebug's mother haunted him during the waking hours of the coming winter, but at night the image of the star maiden drifted through his dreams. Often he would stand in the dark wrapped in a blanket, away from the warmth and light of lodge fires, staring up at the night sky. Often it would seem like a star had moved, but then he'd see it hadn't moved at all.

Though Eshkebug was preoccupied with thoughts of the beautiful star maiden throughout that winter, he did not neglect his family or his people. During the cold winter hunts, Eshkebug was especially helpful, for he could change himself into the form of a deer, and attract the one that had to be sacrificed so the People could eat. His ability enabled him to make certain that the hunters killed only what they needed, and that they took the smallest, the slowest, and the weakest. And he always made offerings of tobacco and sang prayers to the spirit of the one who gave his life for the People. Eshkebug would not kill a deer himself; in this way, he kept his medicine gift of transformation strong.

During the Great Mystery Moon, when the surface of the earth is frozen and white, when the water along the shores of Gitchie Gumme is solid enough to walk on, Eshkebug had a wonderful dream. In this dream the great stag appeared, the one who had bestowed the ability of transformation upon him. The magical deer showed him a way that he could lure the star maiden to him when she returned. In the dream Eshkebug was told that in the early spring, when the hardy violets first show themselves in the crevices of rocks, the ship of light would return.

That spring Eshkebug often spent time in the field of flowers, watching the sky for the light of the ship or listening for the lovely sound that gave it flight. He watched the Indian violets blossom and turn shades of purple. He watched as little by little the warmth of a spring sun encouraged other flowers to bloom, until the small field once again became a rainbow of colors. That's when the ship appeared.

Eshkebug listened with anticipation to the strange and beautiful song that guided it over the treetops where it hovered, quiet and still. He could sense it scanning the field and the birch forest nearby for anything human that might be threatening; he knew that they would find nothing like that. They would see only flowers and a little fawn standing alone at the tree line.

When the ship landed, the song that had brought it to the earth ceased, and the star maidens descended to the ground on a blue beam. While they talked and walked among the flowers, the youngest and the prettiest, the one that Eshkebug had fallen in love with, headed for the fawn. Carefully she made her way across the field of flowers toward the birch trees where Eshkebug stood watching from behind the big brown eyes of the sweet little deer.

The star maiden approached the animal, showing the back of her hand so that her long slender fingers pointed down. I mean no harm, she said in the silent language of the mind. As she stroked the soft hair of the fawn's back, she spoke again. You are so beautiful — so gentle. But when she squatted before the handsome young deer and glanced in his soft brown eyes, she recognized something that made her suddenly aware that the attraction found in the eyes of the fawn evoked in her the same feelings she had when she had first seen the handsome human standing with his hand raised in peace but with a weapon by his side.

The star maiden sensed the strangeness of the moment, but she couldn't resist lightly brushing the fawn's silky brow one more time. Then she quickly turned and started back in the direction of her sisters and the ship. But then she stopped and pondered. What was she experiencing? What had just transpired? She took a deep breath to restore her composure, and turned around once again, not knowing what would happen when she did or what she would see.

Instead of seeing the fawn, she saw Eshkebug. She'd been taught to run from humans, but still she hesitated. Eshkebug seized her arm. "Please," he cried, "Don't be afraid!" But it was too late. Fear raced through her mind. She called for her sisters, but before they could react, Eshkebug had disappeared with her into the forest.

For the remainder of the day the starcraft wandered above the treetops, returning to the field of flowers. All that day the craft searched for the young maiden. All that day Eshkebug hid, moving among the trees with the power of the deer, wondering what the beings in the craft might be thinking about a world that could be so lovely and peaceful yet could suddenly turn so disturbing and violent. All that day, until the sun set and the evening star appeared, the craft of light roamed about like a lonely firefly on a cold night. When complete darkness finally descended upon the field of flowers and over the forests of pines and birches, the craft slowly lifted toward the heavens and disappeared among the stars.

Eshkebug returned to his village, the star maiden walking reluctantly behind him, his hand clasped around hers, his force pulling her toward his mother's lodge.

She trembled in the wigwam door as Eshkebug

informed his mother what he had done. His mother shook her head in disbelief, but quickly turned her attention to the young maiden, and invited her closer to the warmth of the fire, and instructed her son to make it stronger.

Her smooth skin glowing in the light of the flames was, indeed, the most beautiful sight Eshkebug had ever seen. She looked around at a strange world. It must have been like becoming conscious in a dream. At first she shielded herself from the touch of Eshkebug and his mother. But then Eshkebug's mother offered her a cup of broth, and the maiden took it.

As she sipped from the copper cup and as the broth warmed her inside, her trembling slowly ceased. Her eyes swept around the room, examining the articles and utensils in the lodge, and her gaze fell on the man sitting a distance away from her.

"Don't be afraid," Eshkebug said, but the strange words had little effect on the young star maiden.

Eshkebug hoped that even though she could not understand the words, she could feel the good intent in their sound. Though she had stopped shivering, the star maiden still appeared afraid. Eshkebug looked at his mother. Desperation filled his eyes. "I had given all my thoughts toward her capture. I had not considered the consequences."

Eshkebug's mother squatted near the star maiden, contemplating the dilemma. Gently, she took the half-empty cup of broth and offered her a feathered pillow and a cattail mat to sleep on. "Eshkebug, my son, you've frightened this young maiden nearly to death." His mother turned to him. "How can she trust you after what you've done?"

The star maiden laid down on the mat and closed her eyes. "She's probably hoping to wake up from this dream, Eshkebug. But she won't be able to. Now you will have to show her that your love is worthy of her sacrifice. I hope you can."

At dawn, Eshkebug held out his hand to her, offering her food. She was hungry, but did not accept it. She did, however, accept the offering from his mother. Then she slept again, hoping it all to be a dream from which she would awaken.

But that was not to be. Every time she opened her eyes, she became more aware that this was now her physical reality. Every time she opened her eyes, Eshkebug was nearby with desperate and saddened deer eyes. He wanted in some way, in any way, to please her, to make her smile. But it was Eshkebug's mother who finally encouraged her to move about. For the first moon of her captivity, she spent much time with Eshkebug's mother, learning what she could about living the life of an earth woman. Eshkebug's mother tried to make her feel more comfortable in her new world by singing songs of life to her.

It wasn't long before the star maiden was given a name. They called her Geezhigoquea, Sky Woman.

For the remainder of that spring and well into the summer, both of Eshkebug's parents helped Sky Woman adjust to her new life. They forced nothing on her, and she slowly overcame her shyness and showed interest in learning all she could. Eshkebug's mother enjoyed the company of the star maiden. She enjoyed having someone to share the work. She enjoyed knowing that her son had chosen a good wife, even though she came from another people and another world. And always Eshkebug would return from a hunt with love and gentleness for the young woman he loved. Sky Woman was surrounded by loving and kind people, and she eventually accepted Eshkebug's offering. A year passed, and they married. A year later she gave birth to a son they called Zhawano-geezhig, Blue Sky.

To the amazement of the small village, she seemed to love Eshkebug, whose whole life centered around her. The people regarded her as one of them and gave her the respect given to any woman of the People, especially one whose heart was good and kind.

As Blue Sky grew, he became increasingly curious about the origin of his mother and about the strange world she came from far away in the stars. The more questions he asked, the more Sky Woman remembered, and it was those memories that caused her to toss and turn at night, disturbing the sleep and the mind of her husband. It was the memories that he would see in her eyes behind the love she showed for him, and it revealed a sadness that hurt Eshkebug to see. He tried showing her the beauty of this earth, taking her into the forests, walking with her in the fields of sweetgrass and flowers. He took her in his canoe along the shore of the Great Water. He showed her everything beautiful about this world, but nothing he could say, nothing he could do could make the loneliness his beautiful wife endured go away.

Then an idea came to him. For weeks he worked at creating a lodge similar to the starcraft that Sky Woman traveled in. When he was done and showed it to her, she wept, and her tears were of joy, not sorrow, for she was truly aware of such an act of love.

Sky Woman spent much time in the lodge that resembled a starcraft. She did almost all of her work in there, and would often fall asleep and dream about her sisters and her parents and of the world she missed so much. And though she tried to conceal this longing before the loving eyes of her husband, he could still see it deep within her. It hurt him to know that her longing would never go away, but that was the warning his mother had given him, the same warning that had been given to her and to her mother: Do not fall in love with a being from the stars.

During a long winter night, when Eshkebug was away hunting, Sky Woman and Blue Sky talked about her world — a world that he too felt a longing for. "Mother, please sing the flight song for me," he said, "the one you said enabled you to come here."

At first, Sky Woman refused, explaining that such a song had great power and that it could only be sung by women. But her son pleaded, and she gave in. "Promise that you will never sing this song," she said. Blue Sky nodded, saying that he would never sing it, that he just wanted to hear it.

Sky Woman closed her eyes and started singing. Images of her family drifted through her mind. She sang until the images became so vivid that she felt them close to her, calling her.

A few nights later Eshkebug returned from the hunt, but no one was in the lodge. He went to the place where he had built the starcraft, but it was gone. He rushed to the lodge of his parents, and they told him what had happened. All night they had heard Sky Woman singing. They said that the song was beautiful. Everyone in the village talked about it the next day. That night was very cold, they said. The sky was so clear it seemed that you could almost touch the stars. They said a bright light floated over the village. Many of the People were frightened and remained in their lodges. Eshkebug's parents peeked outside and saw a blue beam connecting the starcraft that Eshkebug had built to another ship above. They said that as amazing as the incident was, everyone went back to sleep. "Strange," they said. "So strange." The next morning when the village awoke, Eshkebug's mother went to visit her grandson and Sky Woman, but she found nothing there. "Nothing," she said. "The starcraft that you had made for her was gone and so was your wife and son."

Eshkebug was devastated. His whole world crumbled down on him. He ran into the woods and cried for many days.

Meanwhile, among the seven dancing stars, a great celebration was happening, for Sky Woman's father had heard the flight song of his daughter and had sent a ship to get her, for they had never stopped searching for her. They only needed to hear the song.

When she arrived with Blue Sky on her world, she was filled with a joy she had almost forgotten. She hugged her mother and father and wept in their arms. She hugged her sisters. They were reunited once again and celebrated by singing and dancing in the air.

The young Blue Sky was introduced to his grandparents, who quickly wanted to show him everything about their world. Each of his mother's sisters wanted to hold him and play with him. They took him to strange and wonderful places. They showed him where the ancestors on his mother's side lived and told him the stories of their origin and evolution.

But Blue Sky began to miss his father.

He told his mother that he couldn't sleep, for he was haunted by the image of his father weeping. "I need to be with him, Mother. Can we go and get him, and bring him here ... to this world?"

Sky Woman's father warned against such a thing. "No human has ever been to our world," he said. But then he would gaze into the dark eyes of his grandson and see the pain.

"I am human too, Grandfather. I am connected to the Earth as well as this place."

Sky Woman's father finally agreed. In a few days he prepared a ship, and they left together: Sky Woman, her father, her son, and a few others to help along the way. They left to the beautiful sound of the women singing.

When they arrived on Earth, Sky Woman directed

the craft to the field of hardy violets where she had first seen Eshkebug disguised as a beautiful fawn. He was still there, standing among the flowers, only now he was a very old man.

"Eshkebug?" she called, but he did not hear her. "Eshkebug, is that you?" This time he turned around very slowly.

His eyes squinted to see more clearly the origin of the sound of his name. It was not like the other times, he thought, when he would hear his name in the wind or in a dream. This time the sound was alive and he was awake.

The starcraft behind the image was a blurry bright light.

"Eshkebug," the star maiden cried, running to the arms of the old man who was her husband. When they embraced, Eshkebug understood why he'd chosen to stay alive all these years. "But why did you leave me?" he quivered. "Why did you take our son, and leave me all alone, all these years? What cause had I given you?"

What had happened is one of those things that can happen when two worlds come together. The potent warnings of the old ones from both worlds could not prevent this love, but nevertheless the warnings came true, for Sky Woman, in her joy at being reunited with her family, had forgotten that time doesn't work the same way when traveling through the ocean of space. Though she and Blue Sky were gone no longer than one moon, many years had passed on the earth. And all that time Eshkebug had lived with an empty sadness that marked the years of his life. Season after season, year after year he looked to the seven stars, until he could no longer distinguish them from the countless others or even see them at all.

When Sky Woman explained what had happened, Eshkebug fell relieved into her arms. Tears streamed down his old cheeks, for he knew at least his wife had not deserted him intentionally. A great weight was lifted from him, a weight that had bent him heavy with grief and age.

Eshkebug left with Sky Woman and his son, and journeyed to a planet far away in the constellation we now call the Pleiades.

As the candle melted to a small puddle of wax and the shadows merged with the night, Carises and his brother and sister went to sleep peacefully, unfrightened by the idea of visitors from other worlds and faraway star systems. For I had done what the ghost voice of Uncle Nip had advised: I turned to the literature of the People, and the primal wisdom of story. Now my children can go to bed at night, knowing that they have ancestors among the stars. Now, we can only hope that the Star People can hear our songs, like they could hear the flight song of the star maiden . . . now, when we need them.

CHAPTER 5

Old Ways

Some stories need to be told because they preserve the link with previous generations.

— Marc Allen
in *Native Heart*

Stories nourish cultural identity. They help us understand more about who we are and where we came from.

Uncle Chuck showed up on our doorstep one autumn afternoon, a duffel bag hung over his shoulder, a warm smile stretched across his weather-worn face. He stepped inside carrying stories.

Uncle Chuck was my wife's uncle and the great-uncle to our children. He was Simone's mother's brother. He and Simone's mother, Elaine, were as close as any brother and sister could have been. After Elaine's death to ovarian cancer, Uncle Chuck's pain sent him spiraling down. He tried to lose himself, first to alcohol, then to the winds of the four directions. The death of his older sister devastated him, but it also provided him the chance to evaluate his life.

After a gut-wrenching self-evaluation, Uncle Chuck walked away from a generous salary working at a major corporation, a big bank account, and a nice house in the suburbs. He walked away from the people who connected him to that life.

After the death of his sister, Uncle Chuck turned his back on the materialistic and civilized world. He turned his back on what his life had become and set out to find what he wanted it to be. In a way, Uncle Chuck was repeating history, but not in that doomful way where foolish people repeat the mistakes of the past. He had learned from the passing of time, even if it wasn't a conscious effort, but rather from an urging in his primal blood. For he was only imitating what the ancient Mayans had done long ago.

It has been told by tribal elders that when the Mayan priests recognized how urban life had affected their people's connection to Mother Earth and to each other, when they saw what the People had lost spiritually because of what they had acquired materially, the priests convinced an entire nation to walk back into the dark green jungle. My Uncle Nip used to tell me that such an act would be the equivalent today of the entire population of the metropolitan Tampa Bay area overnight packing what they could carry on their backs and walking off toward the forests of Ocala or the wetlands of the Everglades.

Even though Uncle Chuck was only one man, his act, like the Mayans and others before him, had repercussions that went far beyond the circle of his life. It was the ideal and the intention embedded in that act that transubstantiated his act and allowed it to endure in the blood of another generation. He too walked away, only he headed for a bus station in downtown Minneapolis where he purchased a one-way ticket as far as his money would take him, and boarded a Greyhound heading south. All he carried was a few extra dollars, a change of clothes in a rolled-up sleeping bag, and his medicine stone, which he kept wrapped in deerskin in his front pants pocket. When the bus ride ended, Uncle Chuck started walking. None of us knew for sure nor had we asked him, just how far he had walked, or for how many days, or even weeks. We just knew that one sunny autumn afternoon he wound up on the doorstep of our home on the Gulf Coast of Florida.

The children were in awe of him, yet felt so comfortable around him. It was as if Uncle Chuck had lived just down the road and had visited a hundred times before, even though this was the first time they had met. The children loved him. So did Simone, for she could see so much of her mother in him. I loved him too, for he represented that connection to another generation of Ojibway people, a generation that belonged to our children's grandma, to Simone's mom, and to my mother-in-law. He was the new link to the generation that ovarian cancer had denied us.

In the days that followed, he encouraged Carises to

develop his art by teaching him to work with clay, and he reassured our daughter Calusa that she was an exquisite beauty. He acknowledged her blessing, which is the ability to work with sick or wounded animals and birds. He turned our oldest son Ihasha on to classical music like Beethoven and Bach. And he told Simone more about her mother's childhood and about the encounters they too had with the Star People.

I remember late one night how the children struggled to stay awake during one of his stories. Their eyes closed, but their eyelids twitched, like they were dreaming, though I knew that they were more than likely reacting to his voice and his stories. I remember that night most vividly because he told a story about the time he'd spent with a Mayan medicine man. He pulled the small deerskin bundle from his pocket and unwrapped it to reveal his sacred red stone. He showed it to Simone and me before telling the story. I can still see the images of the temple steps and the star designs etched on the sides of the crimson stone's smooth surface. Uncle Chuck explained how the stone connects him to that dream-time when he stood alongside a star-being at the base of a great Mayan pyramid. "It happened when I was a boy," he said, "living on the Rez on White Earth."

As the children drifted in and out of sleep, he told us that the Mayan medicine man he had met a few years back also kept a sacred stone, only this one was the size of a man's hand. He described how the medicine man told him that inside the stone was where he kept his medicine. Uncle Chuck said, "I wasn't sure what he was talking about, until I watched him put his hand inside the stone and take his medicine out." He said that the old shaman described the stone as a living thing. "What the medicine man did was put his hand into the space between the molecules.... That was the space where he kept his medicine. It's another dimension."

There were other stories. Stories about the family, about the times he'd spent with Elaine and his youngest sister, Mira. Times of joy. Times of pain. Times of separation. He knew stories about Simone's family, ones that connected her and the children to the past. He knew stories about Grandma LaRoque.

It was in Grandma LaRoque's garage in Minneapolis where Simone would hide from the sisters at Holy Rosary when she was a young girl. Simone told how every chance she could, she'd sneak out of grade school and hole up for the day with her novels and other storybooks inside Grandma LaRoque's garage. "That's where I read *Island of the Blue Dolphins*," she said, running her fingers through Calusa's silky hair.

Even on those frigid Minnesota winter mornings, Simone would head out for Grandma LaRoque's house and slip inside her cluttered garage where she'd wrap up in a blanket and read. Sometimes her grandmother would see her coming and invite her pretty granddaughter inside for cookies and hot cocoa. These were some of the few memories from childhood that Simone treasured. We laughed at Uncle Chuck's recounting of those times when the nuns would visit Grandma LaRoque's house, searching for that "mischievous little Indian girl with the long black hair, the one who's always reading." We laughed again when Simone recalled the nuns telling the old woman how her granddaughter was under the influence of the devil. "Reading all those books is a dangerous sign," they said.

Uncle Chuck brought many stories back to life when he came to visit years ago on that warm autumn afternoon. He reminded us that human beings are made of stories, and that special stories still exist that have a lasting and unusual effect on us. We ponder the meaning of such stories. We wonder about them. We can never forget them. They haunt us in a way, stirring something in our primal subconscious that intrigues and frightens, fascinates and disturbs.

The story of the six fingers is such a story, for Uncle Chuck's retelling of it during his stay at our home created a prolonged and eerie effect on each of us. Maybe this is because the story reminds us to never take for granted the love of another person. Maybe it was because such a story shows how powerful such love can be — that it is not something to take lightly, but something to respect in an honorable way, something that can be passed down from generation to generation. Or maybe the story of the six fingers simply made us better aware of how powerful the Old Ways really are....

It is in the spirit of the oral tradition that I have presented the accounts that led up to the night Uncle Chuck first told us the story of the sixth finger. And now, my rendition of the story.

The Story of the Six Fingers

Maggie watched from the front step. In the distance she could see him pass through the line of trees that marked the border of her father's property in Nay-tah-waush. He stood among the birches like a great stag, watching her.

Maggie's mother warned her to stay clear of him, warned her that he was probably from White Earth, that he practiced midé. She said that he had most likely left a charm to cause a young girl to fall in love with him. This frightened her mother, for the Midewewin was once a healing society of good-hearted people whose code required them to honor women, for honoring women enabled them to honor the gift of life and love. But that had changed. Over the years, petty jealousies crept into the minds of some who entered the sacred Midewigun (lodge), and they began using the midé to hurt their enemies. It wasn't long before its reputation evoked fear among many of the People. But Maggie had just returned from the Indian boarding school at Chellaco, where her teachers made sure that she learned the evils of such superstitious and pagan beliefs. For that was her teachers' obligation: to civilize the Indian children by "destroying the savage while saving the human."

Yet on summer nights Maggie would listen to his
singing. It would come to her like a lullaby and cause
her to dream about him — about his strength and his
power. Once in a dream she almost surrendered to the
song, for its melody drifted into her unconscious softer
than a whisper through the trees. She glanced down in
the dream and saw a black shawl draped over her shoulders. She saw a black dress wrapped about her small
waist. Each article felt as light as down feathers. She
stood before him, feeling free and warm, the heat of
blood and energy moving across the soft Ojibway skin
of her smooth belly, down toward the small mound at
the base of her abdomen. The same sensation flowed
like hot liquid streams up from her knees into her thighs.
Just as the two forces were about to merge, her mother
heard her daughter stirring and woke her before anything could happen.

On sunny days Maggie would watch him from the
front door, dancing through the shadows of the birches
and chanting songs without words, the kind that could
evoke strong feelings in a listener. Once she nearly left
her home and headed for the tree line, but her mother
had seen him too and stopped her daughter before
Maggie had reached the front step.

One cool summer morning, when Maggie stood, ax
in hand at the wood pile, he appeared. He seemed old to
her, yet she was attracted to him and not afraid of him.
He told her, in the old language that her parents still
spoke, that he loved her, and that he wanted to marry
her. He told her that he would be a faithful and good

husband. Maggie laughed. How could he love her and want to marry her? He didn't know her. He didn't even speak English. He probably didn't even have a job that paid him money.

The handsome man did not return her laughter. Instead, he placed his hand upon the stump that was used to split wood. He told Maggie that his heart was sincere. Then he spread his fingers apart to prove his trusting intent. At first, Maggie smiled, amused by the gesture. Then she looked into his eyes. They were dark quiet pools that reflected her gaze. Suddenly, she felt herself fall into them. That's when she remembered what her mother had told her about the charm. That's when she remembered the teachings at Chellaco about the evils of such primal men who live in superstition and ignorance. She shook her head as if to clear it. Then she motioned with the ax toward his hand. It was a silly girl's gesture to see if he would remove it. He didn't. That's when she pretended to drop the ax.

But she could not stop the force of its weight as it fell. She could only redirect the blow. When she stared down at his hand, she saw how the ax had severed his little finger. She saw the finger laying in the dirt among the wood chips and the blood oozing from the hand down the stump. Her mouth opened and her eyes went wide with horror.

Maggie watched him disappear among the shadows of the birch trees like a wounded deer, and she never saw him again.

Although years later she would abide by church and

government standards and take on the last name of another man, Maggie LaRoque grew to retain dignity as one of the last Ojibway matriarchs.

Before her birth, Maggie's mother had insisted that her husband build a wigwam. She wanted her daughter to be born in a circle. She knew that the houses of civilized men in Nay-tah-waush were all squares. She said that she didn't want to give birth in such a place because a spirit can get trapped in a corner. In this way, the spirit of Maggie would never be trapped by the civilized world.

So, Maggie's birth took place in a wigwam. It happened just before the 1890 massacre of Lakota ghost dancers at Wounded Knee. That massacre epitomized white Americans' brutal attempts at physical genocide, for no other civilized people in the world can claim the extirpation of 1,700 (and counting) indigenous nations. Maggie's birth seems to represent the failure of that genocide, and the beginning of another form of genocide.

As a young child she would witness the indignities of civilized religions. As an old woman she would recount with detail how the missionaries came. How they bickered and argued over Indian souls. How government officials stepped in to stop the squabbling. "They brought us all together and lined us up in rows," she'd say. "They divided us up into denominations in this manner, saying, 'This row is Baptist. This one Methodist. This one Catholic.'" That's when the Ojibway people became fragmented. That's when Ojibway no longer meant The Way that people lived and how they saw the world. "We could no longer gather in groups, except to go to church," she said. "Ceremonies were forbidden.... We couldn't even have a giveaway unless it was Christmas." She explained how anyone caught violating the rules was imprisoned. That was the beginning of their cultural genocide.

As a young girl Maggie was taken from her parents by force. Government agents, Bureau of Indian Affairs police, and ministers of the Judeo-Christian God kidnapped the Reservation children and herded them off like cattle to Chellaco. It was at Chellaco that the genocide would continue. As an old woman she would tell stories about the brutality of government teachers and of those times when Indian children were beaten for speaking the old languages, when Indian children were punished for participating in the old rituals, when Indian children killed themselves out of despair, humiliation, and loneliness.

And though Maggie would endure all this, she couldn't avoid the effects of cultural genocide. For she survived the U.S. Government's forced relocation of her family to Minneapolis and became the mother of nine children and the grandmother to generations, yet she withheld from the young what she knew that was old.

She withheld from teaching those things of her culture that had sustained her people tens of thousands of years. And though she still spoke to her husband in the old language, and still gathered plants for healing in the Old Way, Maggie LaRoque felt that her children would be better off living in the civilized world, and would suffer less if they learned to speak only English and learned little about the Old Ways of the Indian world. And so, like other young native women of those times when centuries and ways of seeing were changing, she gave birth to a "lost generation," those who lived in neither world, those who would often discover that alcohol could help fill the void between both worlds. The jails in the city, the beds in the detox centers, and the cemeteries back on the reservation filled. During Maggie LaRoque's lifetime, the Old Ways were nearly lost, cultural genocide almost completed, and the trap of the civilized world all but realized.

Yet, Maggie was born within the circle, and for the nearly ninety years of her life, she was connected to it, and despite the desperate efforts of civilized-thinking humans to tear her from it even after her death, they could not. For it stands that even until this day, like some midé gesture of primal consciousness, there is, in each generation, a male of Maggie's blood who is born with a sixth finger. It has been said that perhaps the sixth finger is a reminder to each generation of the power in the Old Ways, of the strength there is in the Old Ways, of the reality that still exists in the Old Ways — and the reality that the Old Ways still exist.

CHAPTER 6

The Cord: Primal Child, Civilized World

If today I had a young mind to direct, to start on the journey of life...I would for its welfare...set that child's feet in the path of my forefathers. I would raise him to be an Indian.

— Luther Standing Bear

Primordial passion enabled him to be conceived, but his conception went beyond the sensual and sexual moment when two beings fulfill their creation parts, when their blood exchanges energy and experiences renewal, when they fall away to blissful rest. His conception was deliberate. It was intentional. So the Old Ways would continue.

The summer night when he became a unique entity, created out of the need we had to survive, a star fell across a hazy sky. It was a magnificent sight over the still waters of Lake Calhoun, one not ordinarily seen in the city of Minneapolis, where artificial lights have obscured the stars. His mother truly believed that his spirit was that falling star coming to earth. His mother believed in the Old Ways....

In the autumn she looked so beautiful, pregnant with new life. She always seemed so happy. I can still see her standing on the snowy steps of our small rented house on 19th Avenue. She was wrapped in the poncho I had given her for her birthday. Big, freshly fallen snowflakes decorated her long, luxurious raven hair. A smile parted her full lips, melting the coldness that had too often lingered around my heart.

At peace-time I made him a cradle board of cedar wood. It felt feather light in my arms. She made a small turtle bundle where we would one day keep his umbilical cord. The old ones said that if we did not do these things, our child could spend his life searching for something, always searching.

Her laughter serenaded his slumber in the waters of her womb. I don't think she ever cried while he was inside her. I never gave her reason to cry. I wonder if she's crying now.

On winter days she would tell our unborn child stories of his great-uncles Nippawanock, Star that Rises to Greet the Dawn, and Metacomet, Shooting Star. On arctic nights she would read to him about the heroes of his people: defenders of their children, protectors of the earth, keepers of the Old Ways.

She sang to him often: songs about our love for the land, songs about our connection to all that is sacred.

Sometimes I drummed and sang other songs with her, songs without words but with feeling that made him stir inside her. I wonder if he could hear me singing his name.

She dreamed he was deformed. Something was wrong with the development of his feet; they would be crooked. She dreamed a ceremony for him with all the ancestors present. They gathered in a great circle and sang for him. "I was singing too," she said. They told her they needed time to fix him. He needed time to heal.

When he didn't come out when he was expected to, the doctors and the midwife became concerned. A full moon passed. Another waxing crescent appeared. The icy city lakes began to crack. Though we had trained to bring him naturally into this world, we learned that it wasn't to be. We were afraid.

One day we were told that he must be taken to a hospital — too much time had passed. That night I took the rain rattle, and I shook it over his mother's womb. I shook it all night and at dawn he stirred and kicked and broke the water sack. She felt the water flow and stared at the puddle on the wooden floor. "It's time," she said.

She labored twenty-seven hours in a stark hospital room without drugs of any kind. She wanted him to be born pure. I cooled her with an eagle-feathered fan. I whispered to her that I loved her, and I never left her side, for it was becoming clear that something was wrong. His head had grown too hard over the time it took the ancestors to heal his crooked feet, and it would not pass through the tunnel toward the light of birth. He could not pass through into life without causing his mother's death. So I watched her suffer unimaginable pain while she tried to give birth. I watched her weaken until she almost died.

When they finally cut her open and pulled him out, I took hold of him immediately. That was her last conscious wish: that familiar hands and eagle feathers touch him first. I placed the Great Mystery Pipe in her room, where it would remain until she was ready to leave. As I think back to that time, I may have been the first father to ever participate in a cesarean birth in this civilized country, for all I know. I'm certain it was the first time that eagle feathers and a sacred pipe were ever present during a delivery in that particular hospital.

From the window in the hallway I could see the setting sun. It felt like it was lingering to savor the first warm day of the year. Melting snow was flowing in streams down city streets. Inside the sterile surgery room I held onto my newborn child, and watched in horror as the life-blood poured from his mother. It gushed like a red river until it gathered in a pool that extended from her long coal-black hair to her small moccasin-brown feet.

She nearly died to give him life. Life meant so much to her. I wonder what she would think now.

I took his placenta as the Old Ways teach us and headed down the cold, slippery trail to the Mississippi. March winds howled across the icy, rippling water. There on the river bank, where his mother and I had acknowledged our love for the first time, I dropped the sack of sustenance into the water rapidly moving south and thanked the Mystery and the Earth for the strength of my wife and the new life of my son.

It was as though his birth had fueled a fire already raging in me, and I fought even harder against those who would mock or exploit the race he inherited. I stood my ground against those who would hurt the growth of all my native children. For now I had a Red Nation son!

We brought him home to the Land-Where-the-Wind-Is-Born, the turquoise water place of tall palms and pines, when he was still a baby. He met his great-uncles then. How they loved him!

We called this one, the first born son, Ihasha. Uncle Nip cried out, "Victorious Voice!" We wanted this primal boy-child one day to become his name. We wanted him to carry this name as old as the ancestors. We wanted him to keep their memory alive and to evoke the ancient sleeping spirits with the sound of his name. I wonder if they are aware in the Mystery. I wonder if in some small way there is some kind of collective awareness in the world of spirit.

We walked with him in our arms on the beach of bone-white sand and put him in the Gulf of Mexico when he was six-weeks-old. We introduced him to the sea. It was the Old Way of doing things. We propped him up against a sand dune among morning glory vines and tall golden sea oats. We shaded him from a tropical sun with palm fronds while we played, husband and wife, mates for life, in the salt water womb of the Earth.

I wonder what the spirit of his mother knows now.

Is it a conscious knowing? I wonder if this is how she remains alive, in these memories I have of our lives together, and in that primordial way of passing ancestral genes on to him.

I wonder if she ever knew within her inner self that she would die so young.

What has happened to the Old Ways, my love?

My thoughts to her on quiet nights, while I hold my pipe, explore the Mystery for him.

Can the Old Ways of seeing things continue even as the new ways lure him with the pop music of angry voices and threatening attitudes, even as he interacts with cigarette-smoking, alienated peers, disillusioned and discontented with the artificial world they are inheriting, but clueless how to make it better? She once affectionately called them "rebels without a clue."

Can the Old Ways survive the shadow people who still steal away the spirits of innocence and beauty, just as they did five hundred years ago? Am I powerless to stop them, my love? I can't seem to stop them. I can't keep them from our son.

Can it be true, my love? As he approaches his eighteenth year, I must prepare to cut that second cord, the one we cannot see. I must allow him to walk in whatever world he chooses. I must cut the second cord! But then will the ancestral cord that binds him to the Old Ways be cut, too? Will the turtle bundle that protected the first cord lose its meaning? Will the Old Ways be nothing then? If he is changing, Oh, Great Mystery, be not too hard on him.

Once, near death, she told me, coming out of a dream, that this world in which we live is at best an illusion. I tell our son that if he can't survive in this illusory place as a native person, then he is not really alive. He can become yet more evidence of a culture that is dying. I tell him that if he loses touch with his tribal self, if the Old Ways are nothing, then why did we struggle so hard to keep them? Why did his mother hold the sacred pipe on her death bed? She was so weak she could barely lift it to her lips, but she did and she smoked with her husband and her children in the last days of her life.... Can the Old Ways be nothing?

The seduction process of this civilized world is set in motion. The shadow people draw closer to the innocence of our firstborn child. Only now their shadows are disguised in light. They come glittering and bright. They come with herbs once used to heal and help — tobacco, marijuana, coca. And though their seduction may be slow, the death they cause is as brutal as ever.

While I smoked my prayers today at sunrise and sent my words for him into the sky, I saw a sign that troubled me. I watched a flock of robins gather in the oak across the way. This winter day was born to their voices. The crisp morning air vibrated with their singing. As a cloud drifted across the emerging sun, a silence swept over us and the air became still. As if it appeared out of nothingness, a hawk shot out of the peaceful morning light toward the quiet branches of the oak, like a feathered arrow. His shadow did not go before him. Then, like a down pillow torn apart, the great tree burst into feathers flying in all directions. But one winged one was too slow, and the hawk struck.

As I gripped the pipe tightly and watched, I wondered if my son could feel my prayers for him. But isn't that the magic of the word — that it has the power to be heard by the unseen — that it has the power to make things happen? Yet magic requires faith. Am I questioning my faith? Am I questioning the validity of the Old Ways because I wonder if my son listened to his beating heart today? Does he know that I am singing for him with my drum, just as I did with his mother when he was growing in her womb? Can he hear his own victorious voice above the lies and propaganda of the civilized world, above all the noisy machines of industry and waste, above all the static from televisions and radios? I wonder if the spirits of those who loved him know that I implore them now to help him as the ending of this cycle of his life draws near and the beginning of a new one approaches.

Tonight with feathered prayer stick and sacred pipe I feel the magic of belief as I sit in darkness with my son, within the lodge of red glowing stones. It is the most ancient of the rituals. He speaks strong words. It is as the Old Ways have shown.

And in the fiery heat of purification, I hear her singing.

ACKNOWLEDGMENTS

Contemplations took over four years to write. After the death of my wife I didn't believe I'd ever write again. But eventually, by sitting down and resuming the writing of this book, I reconnected with her in familiar ways, and in new ways I was just discovering. In essence, my wife Simone shared in all of this, either through our conversations while she was in physical form, through her journals that she left behind, or through her living memory that accompanied me every time I sat down to write. Of course, I must acknowledge my children. Ihasha, Calusa, and Carises Horn have matured into young adults starting to make their own way in the world. Aren't they a major purpose in all this?

Beyond honoring them, I would like to acknowledge the loving support, patience, and suggestions of Marc Allen and Becky Benenate of New World Library. Editing doesn't get any better. My sincere appreciation is also extended to Gina Misiroglu for the work she did on the manuscript in its raw form, helping me to produce a work that I am most pleased with. The contributions of all those at New World Library who helped in this project cannot be adequately measured or expressed. And if my friends and colleagues, Professor DeVera Hewson and Dr. Richard LaManna, hadn't offered their editorial suggestions and recommendations, the excellence I sought to achieve would have been lost. And naturally, my agent and friend, Sandra Martin, has helped make anything I write a reality because she's always believed in my abilities and has encouraged me to work for excellence.

I also would like to extend my gratitude to Kathy Warinner, the cover artist for my last book, *Native Heart*, and this one. She is special to me, for she has managed to capture the spirit of each book and express it through her art. So has my son Carises, whose "thought forms" for *Contemplations* came to him one night out of the Mystery when his mom was close to death.

I would like to thank other writers too, like Basil Johnston, Forrest Carter, and Vine Deloria Jr., for recording the stories and the knowledge of the past. And, of course, the elders, my friends and relatives, who have grown to trust me and share with me that I too may document some of what is old and sacred. And migwitch (thank you) to Dee and Holly Crowfeather for their loving support and spiritual insights that helped to keep me sane and whole after my wife had died, when I felt as though I could have fallen apart, and for the ceremonies in Dee's sacred sweat lodge and those special times when we shared the pipes of love and prayer.

May I also extend my gratitude to Anne Wilson Schaef for her thoughts on this work. I know we share an indigenous relationship to the power of the word and to the land we call Mother.

Lastly, may I extend my sincere appreciation to each of you who has written me over the years about *Native Heart*. Please understand that my life was so intertwined with my wife's struggle for her life, and then with the writing of this book, that I could not answer your moving and wonderful letters. But I've kept them all! Sometimes in the stillness of sleepless nights I read them. They help to remind me that for now I must continue to walk this earth journey. May *Contemplations of a Primal Mind* acknowledge my gratitude to all of you who walk the journey with me.

ABOUT THE AUTHOR

Gabriel Horn, White Deer of Autumn, served as one of the original American Indian Movement (AIM) teachers who helped establish the AIM Survival Schools during the early and mid-1970s. He later became the cultural arts director of the Minneapolis American Indian Center and was nominated for Minnesota's Human Rights Award for his work helping to gain spiritual rights for Native American prisoners.

For the past several years he has presented for the Wisdomkeepers' Program in North Carolina, taught writing and literature in college, and given presentations on writing and the environment for various conferences, schools, colleges, and university programs throughout the country. He has been included in the 1996 edition of *Who's Who of America's Teachers*, and has been invited to hold a seat at the World Peace Council of Indigenous Elders.

He has written numerous books for children, including the award-winning *Ceremony in the Circle of Life,* and, for adults, *Native Heart: An American Indian Odyssey*, which has been used in secondary school and university curricula. He lives on the Gulf Coast of Florida with his three children.